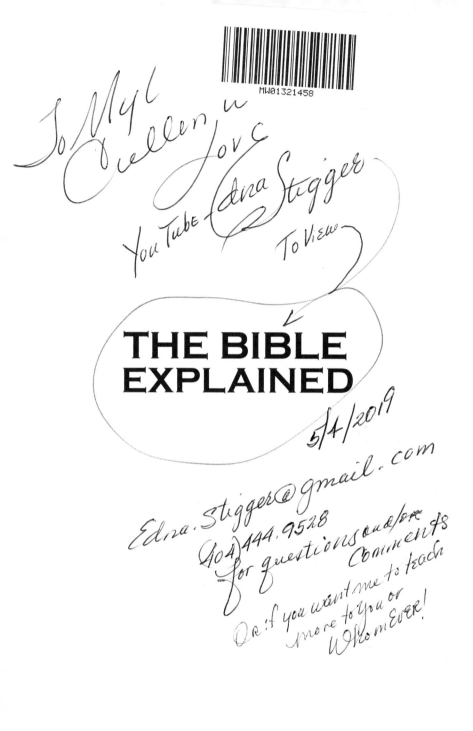

THE BIBLE EXPLAINED

HIS STORY (HISTORY) JESUS CHRIST

A Foundation Bible Teaching and Reference Guide

EDNA STIGGER

XULON PRESS

Xulon Press
2301 Lucien Way #415
Maitland, FL 32751
407.339.4217
www.xulonpress.com

© 2017 by Edna Stigger

Edited by Xulon Press.

All rights reserved solely by the author. The author guarantees all contents are original and do not infringe upon the legal rights of any other person or work. No part of this book may be reproduced in any form without the permission of the author. The views expressed in this book are not necessarily those of the publisher.

Unless otherwise indicated, Scripture quotations taken from the New King James Version (NKJV). Copyright © 1982 by Thomas Nelson, Inc. Used by permission. All rights reserved.

This revision was inspired by Cascade United Methodist Church Elementary Sunday School Students' Memorization of the Books of the Bible.

First Printing: 1996
Second Printing: 2002
Third Printing: 2007
Fourth Printing 2011
Revised 2006 and 2017

Library of Congress Catalogue Card Number: 96–094481
Literary Work United States Copyright: 1994 by Edna Stigger
Registration Number—TXU 668490

(TXU623–809 Sp J/NAD 641–656 Lamb)

www.TheBibleExplained.com

YouTube—Edna Stigger

Printed in the United States of America.

ISBN-13: 9781545611845

Dedicated To

My Children
Charles and Lisa Stigger, and Granddaughter Chanelle Andrea Stigger for their encouragement to proceed with this updated version

My Dear Parents
Eddie and Julia Bland
for raising me in the church

My God-Given Blessed Angel Sisters
Ann Braga and Alice Miles

Some of My Favorite Teachers
Chip Ingram (Chip Ingram APP), Dale Bronner, Adrian Rogers, Tony Evans, David Jeremiah, Chuck Swindoll, Steven Furtick, Ed Young and many other
Atlanta Faith Talk Radio Teachers

Friends and Loved Ones
Charlie, Cagney and Scott Stigger
Matt and Tonya Murphy,
Tracye Miller, Angela Grimes
Reverend Terrilyn Lemons
Reverend Kevin Murriel
Brenda Henderson
Rundu Staggers
Fred Duckett
Reneathia and Nadia Baker
Janet Adams
Tracie Jamison
Malcolm Saunders
Sam Guilford, Nancy Hutchison
Sheila Moore
Janice McClain
Jo Depp
Shirley Griggs
Eilene Sears
Kathleen Toomey
Carolyn Talley
Greg and Kim Cartwright
Reg Pettus
Winston Carhee
Margaret Bell Dennison
Scott Stigger, Cagney Stigger
Luvern Welch
Victor Grant, Marva Greene

Endorsements

Thank you again for your invaluable contributions of *The Bible Explained*. Your knowledge and skill and obedience are providing a great difference in intentional faith development for countless others.
Rev. Dr. Bernice Kirkland, United Methodist Church
District Superintendent

When I read this book, my eyes were open to the minimal sufferings that we are going through. Jesus took the ultimate suffering for us. This is nothing compared to what he went through. Thus, those women or anyone who dares to read this book will be able to forgive as our Lord and Savior forgives us for the hurt and the pain that we caused.
Jean Officer, Nurse/Caregiver

I was a Muslim before reading *The Bible Explained*. Because I understand the Word of God better, I now know why we worship Jesus, and I am now a Christian. Thank you for making it clear.
Laverne _____, Quality Living Services
for Seniors Bible History Class

(This lady attended only two classes a few months ago and never returned. The other members of the class said the name she gave was Laverne, but they did not remember her last name. Her announcement shocked and left me in a "mini" trance. She may have been an angel. I know, as affirmation, she was heaven-sent.)

Thanks for *The Bible Explained* as it is very easy to read, a useful biblical book for self-help in learning the many scriptures. You have developed a wonderful concept to help Christians of all ages, such as my son and me. I am looking forward to more topics by such a thoughtful and intriguing author like you. Your teachings and method of instruction are highly effective and easy to implement. May God continue to bless you and allow you to share your gifts!

      Regina Mincey, Attorney at Law

The Bible Explained helped me mentally outline and understand the Bible better, and your instruction is wonderful. The book made studying easier and simple. Your writing style is brilliant! I recommend every new convert read this book. I have always been a Christian. However, I wish I had read something this revealing during my transformation period while entering my new life as a born-again Christian. It would have saved me a trip into false doctrines.

    Donald Echols, QLS Bible History Class Member

I have been in the church for eighty-five years and have never understood the Bible nor learned so much as I have since I've been in Ms. Stigger's Bible History Class. Her book and explanations have helped me so much.

        Mattie Parks, Bible History

Ms. Stigger's teaching of the Bible has helped my awareness of what God has done for me all my life. Now I thank God more for His blessing, His mercy, and His love. I better understand and have knowledge of His will and the power to carry it out.

        Robert Davis, Bible History

I have learned so much more about the meaning of the Scripture and how to apply it to my daily living. Now I know so much more about the Bible.

       Cariola W. Jones, Bible History

The Bible Explained is the book I give as a gift to everyone who is expecting a gift from me, even if it simply accompanies another gift. I want everyone to experience the knowledge and understanding I received from reading it. It is a gift from God!

Willie Mcgee, Golf Promoter/Coach Mentor

I learned more about the books of the Bible in forty-five minutes than I had learned in over forty-five years. It never was explained to me. I suggest that you video that lesson so that it can reach audiences that you cannot get to. I believe it will encourage more people to pick up their Bibles. I saw men weep (myself included) by the power of God in the message. It is 6 a.m., and I just had to drop you a note of thanks.

Carl McNair
(Author of *In the Spirit of Ronald E. McNair, Astronaut – An American Hero*)

The Bible Exlained is like a precious jewel. Giving my life to Christ late in life, your book helps me so much in the growth of my relationship with Christ. It helps me stay in God's light and understand the Holy Spirit. For all this, I thank you.

Elaine Crayton, Bible History Class

Prayer of Acknowledgment

F**ATHER, I PRAISE** your Holy Name. Your power is awesome and your greatness is beyond measure. You are the glory in my life.

Forgive me for having been so involved in the world that I was not fully aware of your presence and loving guidance all the while. Forgive me for being prideful. Forgive the sins I committed prior to and while learning to be blindly obedient, humble, and submissive to the Word. Restore anyone who I offended or led astray in my ignorance. I sincerely regret the mistakes I have made, and I thank you for your grace and mercy.

Thank you for allowing me to be broken, so I could be molded and dependent on you. Thank you for making me aware of Your will taking place in my life to transform me day by day. Thank you for making each day an adventure of exciting, joyful childlike anticipation. I recognize your gentle guidance, patience, and presence. Thank you for always giving your angels charge over me. They advise and protect me from the forces of this present darkness, while I continue to learn and grow in your ways. Thank you for my peace and salvation through Jesus.

Deliver me from operating in the flesh. Allow your loving Spirit to consume me, to help me obey and be submissive, so that your redemptive power will rush through me to other lives. Continue to direct my paths toward righteousness so that others might be blessed by the truths that I have found in the Word. Help me to make supplications, prayers, intercessions, and thanksgiving for everyone, including leaders and all who are in high positions so that we may lead a quiet and peaceable life in all godliness and dignity. I know this is right and is acceptable in your sight because it is your desire that everyone be saved and come to the knowledge of the Truth. Grant me your wisdom and understanding.

These things I ask in the precious name of Jesus Christ. Amen.

Your Faithful Warrior,
Edna

Contents

Chapter 1.	Biblical Overview	1
Chapter 2.	The Testaments Explained	7

              General Overview
              The Old Testament
              The New Testament

Chapter 3. Biblical Numbers Explained 53
              Biblical Facts
              Biblical Numbers
              Symbolism of Numbers

Chapter 4. Biblical Trinity Explained 61
              Holy, Holy, Holy – God in Three Persons
              Man made in God's Image – Triune
              Spirit, Soul, Body

Chapter 5. Confirmation 73
              General Confirmation
              Jesus, 100% Man, 100% God
              Jesus is the Way, the Truth and The Life
              The Bloodline of the Messiah

Chapter 6. Spiritual Protection Explained 91
              The Whole Armor of God
              The Sword of the Spirit
              Never-Again List — Prayer A.C.T.S.

Chapter 7. Christ-Esteem, Not Self-Esteem) Explained 113
              Jesus Loves Me
              You Are Special!
              How to Recognize New Age Deception

Chapter 8. **Supernatural Grace** 129
Amazing Grace
Salvation Prayer
The Alpha and the Omega *(The Many Names of Jesus)*
Chapter 9. **Biblical Helps and Exercises** 147
Where to Find It in the Old Testament
Where to Find It in the New Testament
Exercises
Appendix.................................... 159

Contents of Each Chapter of the Old and New Testaments
Psalm and Proverbs References

Foreword

IN THE BEGINNING was the Word (the *Logos*) and the Word was with God and the Word was God (John 1). Millions of persons read, debate, ignore, and even believe this reality. Edna Stigger is one who lives in the reality of the Word of God. She has been given a special gift of interpreting the Word, not only though study but through her own process of spiritual formation. Her witness, through writing, is the result of refusing to be conformed to this world but transformed by a renewed mind (Romans 12:1-2).

God has given Edna a mind to see the Word in practical frameworks. Using acronyms, rhymes, pictorial patterns and even songs, *The Bible Explained* enhances the reader's faith and leaves them with a sense of joy and freedom in being a Christian. When I met Edna, I was amazed to find that she was not on the track to ordained ministry. Not only that, she wasn't interested in such proclamation. She is a gifted and anointed Christian educator, who has overcome by the Word of our Lord and the reality of her personal testimony. Her stumbling blocks have become her stepping stones to God's blessings. She uses her relationship with God to bless countless numbers of others.

The Bible Explained is a clear representation of God, faith, and practice. It is presented in a form conducive to various styles and settings of learning. Children get it. New members cling to it. Young adults are ignited by it. Mature adults appreciate it with a sense of fulfilled

The Bible Explained

expectation after seasons of nebulous understanding. Preachers confirm this partnership in sharing the gospel. God has given Edna a special "code" to crack the Word. She lives it and spends her life giving it to *all* of us. No reader goes unchanged. Each reader passes it on. To God be the glory.

Reverend Dr. Bernice Williams Kirkland
District Superintendent of the United
Methodist Church,
Atlanta College Park District
Ordained Elder in the North Georgia Conference

INTRODUCTION

THE PRAYER OF acknowledgment was necessary to start this work. After that prayer of repentance, the Lord helped me see what was needed by many Christians as a starting point, especially after being saved.

I was born into the Christian faith, baptized as a baby, raised in the Sunday school, and sang in the children's choir and eventually the adult choir. I was married in the church, taught Sunday school and Vacation Bible school, and raised my children in the same "religious" way. Nurtured by wonderful loving parents, I had no idea what was missing in my life—or that I had a need.

My spiritual resume contained the word *Christian*, yet I was not born again until some traumatic circumstances shook me to my foundation. The difference was as great as the darkness of night and the light of day between serving the Lord in my flesh and knowing Him as my personal Savior. As a newly born-again Christian, I knew that something special had happened, yet I needed to know the Word. I had been reading it all my life, but after I experienced a transformation and renewal, the Word came alive. Words I had read for years began to make sense, even though the programming of the world made the biblical principles seem foreign to me.

With no saved mentor, seeking spiritual help and peace, I joined a New Age group. Praise the Lord, I had been studying and knew enough of the Word to finally realize I was being led astray by a false teacher. God delivered me one more time.

After several years of being a "closet" born-again Christian, embarrassed by my previous actions and lifestyle, I repented. The Lord granted me the ability to record the biblical structure that started me on a successful journey toward understanding the Bible and God's will.

It is for this purpose that I was led to create this biblical instruction book entitled *The Bible Explained*. Of course, only the Holy Spirit can explain the Bible, and much will not be understood until we get to heaven. However, I had to make the attempt. Many theologians will not agree with my diagrams, but laymen will understand the Bible better and perhaps be inspired to seek truth for themselves.

It is my joy to teach foundational truths to children, adults, and a very favorite audience, senior citizens, to help them teach others. They testify about the changes that the knowledge and understanding of this material has made in their lives. My prayer is that you will be blessed by it, too.

Since the terrorist's attack on America September 11, 2001, people are looking for peace and a way to not be fearful. God did not give us this spirit of fear. Allow me to introduce you to the Way; my God, the Prince of Peace, Jesus Christ (2 Timothy 1:7).

Jesus Is in Your Clouds. Start Looking Up!

> I have set my rainbow in the clouds, and it will be the sign of the covenant between me and the earth. Whenever I bring clouds over the earth and the rainbow appears in the clouds, I will remember my covenant.... Never again will the waters become a flood to destroy all life. (Genesis 9:13–15 NIV)

Introduction

Many people are unaware of the symbolism of the rainbow. Without frequent church school attendance and/or biblical teaching in the home, how could they know? When the Word is not known, it is easy for the world to use biblical symbolism to stand for its messages without question.

I saw the likeness of this book's cover picture before me on a bright, sunny day. In the midst of everyday business hustle and bustle, God's sign was right there! The honking horns behind me suggested that others may not have seen the rainbow. If they did, there was absolutely no appreciation for it. As I moved on, I praised God for His revealed glory. Although it was there for everyone to see, most people did not. They were not looking up. Normally, neither do I. At that moment, I felt so special.

From Genesis to Revelation, clouds represent the presence, guidance, glory, and protection of God. Here are several of a myriad of scriptural examples:

Guidance: "The LORD went ahead of them in a pillar of cloud to guide them" (Exodus 13:21).

Protection: "The cloud... moved from in front and stood behind them, coming between the armies of Egypt and Israel. Throughout the night the cloud brought darkness to the one side and light to the other side; so neither went near the other all night long." (Exodus 14:19-20)

Glory: "an immense cloud with flashing lightning and surrounded by brilliant light... like the appearance of a rainbow in the clouds on a rainy day, so was the radiance around Him. This was the appearance of the likeness of the glory of the LORD." (Ezekiel 1:4, 28)

Presence: "Clouds and darkness surround Him..." (Psalm 97:2)

"The LORD rides on a swift cloud" (Isaiah 19:1)

"While he [Peter] was still speaking, a bright cloud enveloped them, and a voice from the cloud said, 'This is my Son, whom I love; with Him I am well pleased. Listen to Him!'" (Matthew 17:5)

"After he said this, He was taken up before their very eyes, and a cloud hid Him from their sight.... Jesus... will come back in the same way you have seen Him go into heaven." (Acts 1:9, 11)

"Seated on the cloud was one 'like a Son of man' with a crown of gold on His head." (Revelation 14:14)

My favorite daily devotional, *My Utmost for His Highest*, by Oswald Chambers, (July 29) states:

In the Bible clouds are always associated with God. Clouds are the sorrows, sufferings, or providential circumstances, within or without our personal lives, which seem to contradict the sovereignty of God. Yet it is through these very clouds that the Spirit of God is teaching us how to walk by faith.

If there were never any clouds in our lives, we would have no faith. *"... the clouds are the dust of His feet."* (Nahum 1:3) Clouds are signs that God is there. What a revelation it is to know that sorrow, bereavement, and suffering are the clouds that come along with God! God cannot come near us without clouds—He does not come in clear-shining brightness.... His purpose in using the

Introduction

cloud is to simplify our beliefs until our relationship with Him is exactly like that of a child—a relationship simply between God and our own souls, and where other people are but shadows.

Except for the Bible, reading and journaling in this devotional for the last decade has been the most important supplement to my spiritual growth through difficulties. What difficulties are you facing today? You can be victorious by trusting in God's promises. It is when we are burdened by some seemingly insurmountable problem, such as loneliness, heartbreak, and disappointment that we must dwell on His promises. Memorize Proverbs 3:5–8 for supernatural direction or some other pertinent scripture about trust and faith in God. Faith is the link that connects our weakness to God's strength. Jesus said, "Take my yoke upon you and learn of me; for I am gentle (meek) and humble in heart, and you will find rest for your souls. For my yoke is easy and my burden is light" (Matthew 11:29–30). Whether you *feel* like it or not, pray and praise Him. Take up your *cross* and follow Him (Luke 9:23). Then "Study to show thyself approved unto God" (II Timothy 2:15 KJV).

God has not promised to keep us from life's storms of adversity, but to keep us through them. "In this world you will have tribulation" (John 16:33). "The sufferings of this present time are not worthy to be compared with the glory which shall be revealed in us" (Romans 8:18). But we can "be of good cheer" because Jesus has "overcome the world" (John 16:33). "Blessed are the poor in spirit, for theirs is the kingdom of heaven" (Matthew 5:3).

There is no pain, night, death, or tears in heaven. Jesus said, "Unless you change and become like little children, you will never enter the kingdom of heaven" (Matthew 18:3). Do not be downhearted, beloved child of God. Jesus loves you.

The horrible attack on the World Trade Centers on September 11, 2001, was a wake-up call for America to return to the Word, and many people did.

It was a frightening and incredibly sad time for America. However, it was a blessing to turn on secular media and so often hear the Christian song "Amazing Grace" playing to comfort the masses, "God Bless America" to show the spirit of nationalism and loyalty, and prayer in schools. All these public Christian acts occurred without the negative intervention of the ACLU. Then the 2003 war in Iraq took patriotism to a whole new level, as our troops left to fight in a foreign land in hope of bringing peace. However, the only hope for world peace is the coming of the Prince of Peace. "Peace I leave with you, My peace I give to you; not as the world do I give to you. Let not your heart be troubled, neither let it be afraid.(John 14:27).

Remember the cover of *The Bible Explained*. Allow the simplified Holy Spirit–filled contents of this book to spur you with childlike anticipation to study the Word. Join me on my adventurous journey to learn more about our Lord and Savior Jesus Christ, and expect God to keep His promises. Do you remember seeing more rainbows when you were a child? The sky is vast, still filled with clouds and an occasional rainbow. Just gaze at the heavens to see the Word. Jesus is coming back soon. Start looking up!

Chapter 1

BIBLICAL OVERVIEW

The Heavens declare the Glory of God; and the firmament showeth His handiwork. (Psalm 19:1)

The Bible Explained

Here are the books of the Bible, divided by Old and New Testaments and the divisions of each.

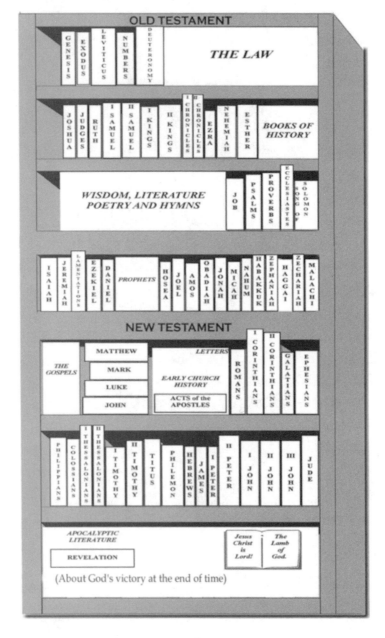

Chapter 1
The Bible is about justice, grace, mercy, and love.

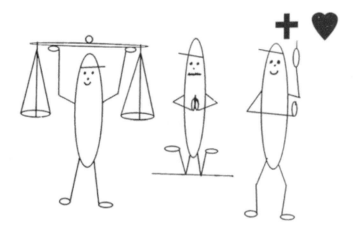

"He has shown you, O man, what is good; and what does the LORD require of you, but to do justly, to love mercy, and to walk humbly with your God?" (Micah 6:8)

The *Old Testament* is the *foundation*.
The *New Testament* completes the *Old*.

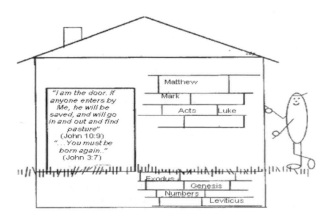

The Bible Explained

The Old Testament

The Triune God is clearly seen in the Old Testament.

Go ye therefore, and teach all nations, baptizing them in the name of the Father, and of the Son, and of the Holy Spirit. (Matthew 28:19)

Chapter 1

For the visible things of him from the creation of the world are clearly seen, being understood by the things that are made, even his eternal power and Godhead; so that they are without excuse. (Romans 1:20)

His Story in the Bible

Watch the Pattern. The last became first, the barren blessed.

ADAM
The son of God — Luke 3:38

Cain and **ABEL** — Genesis 4:4-5
(Adam's Sons)

ABRAHAM
The father of many nations — Genesis 12:2-3; 17:1-27

Ishmael and **ISAAC** - Genesis 17:21
(Abraham's Sons. Sarah, Isaac's mother, was barren.)

Esau and **JACOB** — Genesis 27:30
(Isaac's Sons. Jacob's mother, Rebecca, was barren. Jacob's name changed to Israel)

Leah and **RACHEL** — Genesis 29:30
(Jacob's Wives. Rachel was barren.)

Leah's children and Rachel's Child **JOSEPH** — Genesis 37:3 Manasseh and **EPHRAIM** — Genesis 48:13-20
(Joseph's sons)

Aaron and **MOSES** — Exodus 3:10 Jesse's older sons and **DAVID** — I Samuel 16:12

The Bible Explained

David's firstborn *with Bathsheba,
and* **SOLOMON** — II Samuel 12:24

Job's First and **Latter Blessings** — Job 42:12
John the Baptist and **JESUS** — Matthew 3
*(John's mother, Elizabeth, was barren.
Jesus' mother, Mary, was a virgin until after His birth.)*

The first Adam and the **Last Adam** — I Corinthians 15:45
The Son of God, our God of Grace,

JESUS CHRIST

(Read Romans 5, reconciliation by Christ,
and I Corinthians 15:12–58)

Chapter 2

The Testaments Explained

All Scripture is given by inspiration of God, and is profitable for doctrine, for reproof, for correction, for instruction in righteousness: That the man of God may be perfect, thoroughly furnished unto all good works. (II Timothy 3:16–17)

The Bible Explained

The Old Testament

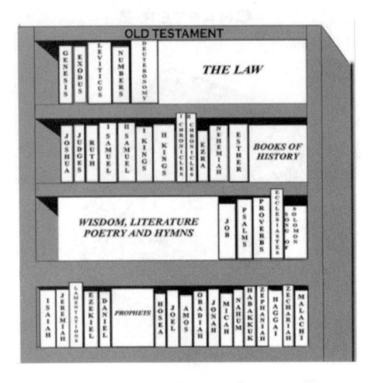

LAMBS – SIN OFFERINGS
(Leviticus 4:32)

Chapter 2

THE LAW

Every major doctrine is in Genesis, this book of beginnings.
1. Where did life come from is in the Creation story.
2. Why there is evil? It is because of the Fall.
3. The first judgment was the Flood.
4. The first promise is seen in the Rainbow.
5. God chose a family: Abraham, Isaac, Jacob, Joseph, and so on.
6. God's plan, through the lineage He chose, was to bring the Messiah, of whom was foretold that one day His heel would be bruised, but He would defeat the enemy (3:15), God's plan is all laid out in the fifty chapters of Genesis.

GENESIS portrays Jesus Christ, Our Creator God

FOCUS:
God created Eden, formed man, and made woman from man's rib. Man was made in God's image—Jesus. The relationship between God and humanity was broken in the garden but restored through sacrifices. Adam and Eve committed the first sin, and God gave them skin coverings for sin. (Blood was shed for that.) (3:21) Man was sent away from the center of the Garden to keep them away from the Tree of Life. Family discord followed.

The Bible Explained

FAMOUS BIBLE STORIES: Disobedience in the garden brought about the Fall of Man. Genesis 3 is pivotal to human suffering because of the punishment connected with the Fall (3:14-19, 22-24) (Eve's punishment was *submission* [3:16], and Adam's punishment was *hard work* [3:17-19]). God sacrificed an animal sacrificed for their covering (3:21). The first family suffers strife when son Cain kills Abel (4:8). Then came more sin and the flood meant to purge the land of sin and the rainbow of promise that followed (6:7-9:17). Sodom and Gomorrah were destroyed for sin (19:1-29). Abraham's sons Ishmael and Isaac (15-22) were the sons of disobedience and obedience. Joseph's story is in Genesis 37-50. He was imprisoned after a false rape accusation (39) *"And the Lord was with Joseph"* statement was repeated numerous times throughout his story.

FAMOUS BIBLE VERSES: *"Let us make man in our image."* (1:26) *"And the Lord God formed man of the dust of the ground, and breathed into his nostrils the breath of life;..."* (2:7)

Exodus Portrays Jesus Christ, Our Passover Lamb

FOCUS:
To bind His people to Him in covenant, using Moses, God delivers them from Egyptian slavery. Stories in Exodus include the Prince of Egypt story; The last plague when the lamb's blood was shed for deliverance from death (12:3-13). This book spotlights God's direct involvement in human history and how God responds to people who trust him.

FAMOUS BIBLE STORIES: Moses' birth (1:8-2:10); the burning bush (3:1-14); the ten plagues (8:1-12:30), the lambs' blood for sin offering; Passover (12); crossing the Red Sea on dry land (14); and the golden calf (32)

Chapter 2

FAMOUS BIBLE VERSES: The Ten Commandments: the first four pertain to our relationship with God; the last six to personal relationships. (20)

Leviticus Portrays Jesus Christ, the Sacrifice for Sin

FOCUS:
Levitical priests explain how to worship God. This book is a worship offering recipe manual. Animal blood was shed as offerings for *temporary* forgiveness of sin as the result of perpetual disobedience, which showed God's mercy to the penitent. The rules of maintaining a relationship with our patient and merciful God were established. Jesus is our High Priest.

Famous Bible Verse: *"the blood... makes atonement"* (17:11).

Numbers Portrays Jesus Christ, Our "Lifted-Up One"

FOCUS:
Due to their lack of faith and commitment, the Israelites wandered forty years in the wilderness. Two censuses were taken; families and individuals were counted. God gave them rules about inheritances and offerings. Animal blood was shed as sin offerings (18:17; 19:5) Jesus is our "cloud by day... fire by night" (9:16).

FAMOUS BIBLE STORY: Moses' punishment for disobedience (20:1–13).

FAMOUS BIBLE VERSE: "The Lord is longsuffering... by no means clearing the guilty, visiting the iniquity of the fathers upon the children unto the third and fourth generation" (14:18).

Deuteronomy Portrays Jesus Christ, Our Prophet

FOCUS:
Moses' address warned the Israelites, reminding them of their history and God's Law. It was a call to the new generation to renew the covenant broken by their parents. The prefix *Deu* means *second telling*. The book is a review, of the first four books.

FAMOUS BIBLE STORY: Designation of Joshua as Moses' successor (31:1-30); Moses' final blessing (33:1-29).

FAMOUS BIBLE VERSES: The Ten Commandments are *restated* in full in Deuteronomy 5; How to raise children to know God (6:4-9).

The Books of History

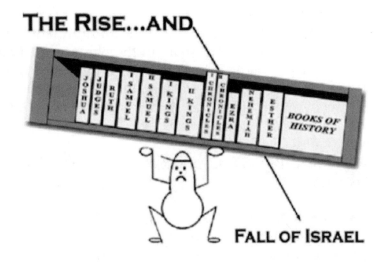

Chapter 2

Joshua Portrays Jesus Christ, Salvation Captain

FOCUS:
The Israelites settled the promised land of Canaan after they captured it. Joshua's faith and obedience bring the wall tumbling down.

FAMOUS BIBLE STORIES: Crossing the Jordan River (3); the Fall of Jericho (5:13–6:27); the prostitute Rahab earns God's protection for hiding spies (2:1–24).

FAMOUS BIBLE VERSES: "Be strong and of good courage; be not afraid, neither be thou dismayed: for the Lord thy God is with thee whithersoever thou goest" (1:9), and "the wall fell down flat" (6:20).

Judges Portrays Jesus Christ, Our Deliverer Judge

FOCUS:
Everyone must face God, as Savior of as Judge. Israelites go through cycles of sin, suffering, salvation. Chastised for disobedience.

FAMOUS BIBLE STORY: Song of Deborah and Barak (4–5); Samson and Delilah (6)

IMPORTANT BIBLE VERSE: Referring to idol worship: "They shall be as thorns in your sides... their gods shall be a snare unto you" (2:2–3).

Ruth Portrays Jesus Christ, Our Kinsman-Redeemer

FOCUS:
God's love, faithfulness, and care are mirrored by this loyal daughter-in-law. Ruth, a foreigner, became Naomi's

closest family member after the death of her husband and sons. The book may have been written to encourage the Israelites to include foreigners in their nation (See Isaiah 56:1-8).

FAMOUS BIBLE STORY: Naomi and Ruth (1-4) (Ruth finally marries Boaz and is David's great-grandmother.) Ruth was obedient.

FAMOUS BIBLE VERSE: "Whither thou goest, I will go… where thou lodgest, I will lodge… and thy God my God" (1:16).

1 and 2 Samuel Portray Jesus Christ, Prophet-King

FOCUS:
The twelve tribes of Israel unite under a king. The Ark is captured. Saul's kingship is described. David becomes Israel' greatest king, but he has major flaws.

FAMOUS BIBLE STORIES: David and Goliath (I Samuel 17); David becomes king, (2 Samuel 5:1-12); David and Bethsheba committed adultery and he engineered the murder of her husband Uriah. Nathan, the priest, tells of God's punishment with the prediction of evil "out of your own house…" (II Samuel 11-12). "Because by this deed thou hast given great occasion to the enemies of the Lord to blaspheme, the child… shall surely die" (II Samuel 12:14). The book shows David's daughter Tamar's was raped by her half-brother Amnon, who was murdered by her full brother Absalom (2 Samuel 13).

FAMOUS BIBLE VERSE: "To obey is better than sacrifice" (I Sam 15:22). Sorrowful and under conviction, "David said… I have sinned against the Lord" (2 Samuel 12:13).

Chapter 2

1 and 2 Kings Portrays Jesus Christ, Our Reigning King

FOCUS:
Israel divides into two rival nations. David's son Solomon was made king. Solomon's wives brought in idolatry; the book includes his blessings and prayer. Both Jewish nations were destroyed for disobedience.

FAMOUS BIBLE STORIES: Solomon is made king (I Kings 1:11–40), and the queen of Sheba visits Solomon (1 Kings 10:1–13). Elijah was fed by ravens (I Kings 17:1–6). David's lineage, including a seven-year-old king, is described (II Kings 11:1–21).

IMPORTANT BIBLE VERSE: David's dying words to Solomon: "I go the way of all the earth: be strong therefore, and shew thyself a man" (I Kings 2:2).

1 and 2 Chronicles Portray Jesus Christ as King

FOCUS:
1 and 2 Kings are chronicled, or recounted. David's son's reigns are analyzed, detailed, and reported in them. Many sons were ungodly, but they were called to recognize their godly roots and rediscover their heritage.

FAMOUS BIBLE VERSE: "There is no God like thee in the heaven, nor in the earth; which keepest covenant, and shewest mercy unto thy servants, that walk before thee with all their hearts" (II Chronicles 6:14).

Ezra Portrays Jesus Christ, Our Restorer

FOCUS:
When the Jews returned from exile, spiritual renewal began. God showed His willingness to offer a second

chance. The book reveals God as the power behind earthly events and contrasts purity with compromise, as well as the lure of secular values.

IMPORTANT BIBLE VERSE: "Ezra had prepared his heart" (7:10).

Nehemiah Portrays Jesus Christ- Builder, Restorer

FOCUS:
The broken walls of Jerusalem are rebuilt by Jews returning from exile. Watch for the ways he balanced his spirituality with down-to-earth action. Example: "We prayed to our God and posted a guard" (4:9).

IMPORTANT BIBLE VERSE: "Think upon me, my God, for good, according to all that I have done for this people" (5:19).

Esther Portrays Jesus Christ, Our Advocate

FOCUS:
Esther, a beautiful Jewish girl, becomes queen and saves fellow Jews, who were like family from slaughter. God delivers His children.

FAMOUS BIBLE STORY: Esther saves her people (2:5–18; 3:12–5:8).

FAMOUS BIBLE VERSE: "I will go to the king… and if I perish, I perish" (4:16). The Book of Esther does not mention God's name.

Chapter 2
WISDOM, LITERATURE, POETRY

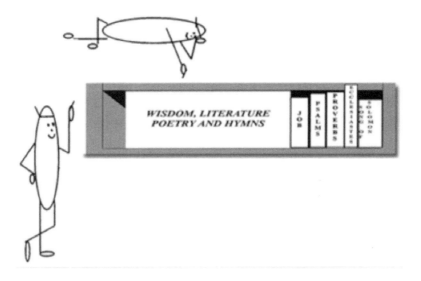

Job Portrays Jesus Christ, Our Kinsman Redeemer

FOCUS:
This book explains why the righteous suffer. Satan petitioned God to strike "perfect" Job with immeasurable losses. His horrendous attempts (including the death of all ten of Job's children) to get Job to sin failed, but his friends' questioning slightly weakened his resolve. Even his wife said, "Curse God and die!" Yet, he did not sin. God allows human suffering for His own purposes.

FAMOUS BIBLE STORY: Job's trials (1–2) and blessings (42) are described.

FAMOUS VERSES: "Man that is born of a woman is of few days and full of trouble (14:1). "And the Lord turned the captivity of Job, when he prayed for his friends: also gave Job twice as much as he had before" (42:10).

Psalms Portrays Jesus Christ, the All in All and the Shepherd

FOCUS:
The Psalms are hymns of praise to our Almighty God during David's run to escape Saul. (Most were written by David, referred to as "a man after God's own heart" due to his conviction and willingness to confess his sins, repent, and praise God. Among the Psalms are confessions, appeals, comfort, protection, and affirmations.) An ancient Jewish songbook, Psalms showcases prayers, praise, and complaints.

FAMOUS PSALMS: 1, 23, 34, 71, 91, 100, 119, 150 — too many to list!

Proverbs Portrays Jesus Christ, Our Wisdom

FOCUS:
The book of wisdom and understanding, addressing his Solomon's son. (The proverbs were mostly written by Solomon, David's son) It includes guidance for the young and encouragement for people to pursue God. It warns against the peril of adultery (5). Chapter 31 contains a long poem in praise of wives. Wisdom is called the *Tree of Life*.

FAMOUS VERSES: Trust in the Lord with all your heart, and lean not to your own understanding." (3:5) Memorize all of 3:5-8).

NOTE: There are 31 chapters in Proverbs and 31days in most months. Read a chapter of Proverbs a day to keep ignorance away and to gain wisdom and understanding.

Chapter 2

Ecclesiastes Portrays Jesus Christ, the End of All Living

FOCUS:
Written from a human perspective, not God's, Ecclesiastes describes the vanity of life and wisdom's protection. Life is unsatisfying and empty, and doesn't make sense without God. Without Him, life is hopeless. The book is an attempt to present the wisdom of living in the moment, enjoying the small joys of life, and relying on the power, presence, and goodness of God to sustain us in our fallen and broken world.

FAMOUS CHAPTER: Everything has its time! (3); the whole duty of man (12:9-14)

Song of Solomon (aka Song of Songs)

Portrays Jesus Christ, Lover of Our Souls, Our Loving Bridegroom

FOCUS:
A picture of God's unconditional love, the Song of Solomon is an allegory of God's love for Israel. It celebrates the gift of love and sexuality and reflects the intimacies of God's *love* with poetic language that conveys feelings more than facts. Married love is a beautiful thing worth celebrating. It is a lovely picture of the physical side of love. Its sensual words applaud sexuality as part of God's wonderful creation. The book is prophetic of Christ and the church. Like the book of Esther, there is no mention of God.

The Bible Explained

The Prophets

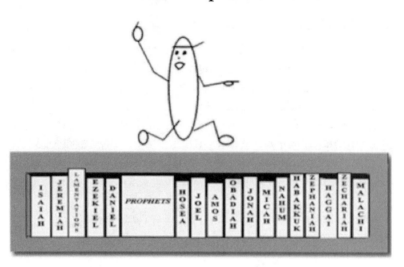

Scriptural Definition of a Prophet

I will raise them up a Prophet from among their brethren, like unto thee [Moses] and will put my words in his mouth; and he shall speak unto them all that I shall command him. (Deuteronomy 18:18)

More Facts about the Books of Prophecy:
- They belong to the dark ages of God's chosen people.
- Prophets were the evangelists of the day, who spoke fearlessly to kings and people alike of their sins and failures.
- The prophetic period covered five hundred years. Then they were silent until John the Baptist.
- There are four major prophets and twelve minor prophets, divided not because of their importance, but because of the length of their books.
- The prophets foretold future events, especially the coming and reign of the Messiah.

Chapter 2

- Prophecy occupies nearly one-third of the Bible

Prophets according to special messages:
Three to Israel	Amos, Hosea, Ezekiel
Two to Nineveh	Jonah, Nahum
One to Babylon	Daniel
One to Edom	Obadiah
Nine to Judah	Joel, Isaiah, Micah, Jeremiah, Habakkuk, Zephaniah, Haggai, Zechariah, Malachi

Jesus' life fulfilled hundreds of prophesies. He was not killed! He could have prayed to the Father to send "twelve legions of angels" for his rescue (Matthew 26:53). He laid down His life and took it up again!

Isaiah Portrays Jesus Christ, the Messiah, the Prince of Peace

FOCUS:
Message: A coming Messiah will save people from sins. God is our Defender!

Messianic Prophecies: "Behold, a virgin shall conceive, and bear a son, and shall call his name Immanuel" (7:14). "For unto us a child is born..." (9:6-7).

Also: 2:2-4; 8:14; 9:6;, 11:1-5, 10; 22:20-22; 28:16; 30:29; 32:2; 33:21; 35:4-6; 40:3, 10-11; 41:14-16; 42:1-7; 45:15, 21; 49:1-2, 7-10; 50:6; 51:9-10; 52:13-15; 53:1-12; 54:5;, 55:4-5; 59:20; 60:3; 62:11; 63:1-3,8-9, 19

Jeremiah Portrays Jesus Christ—Righteous Branch
Lamentations—The Weeping Prophet

FOCUS:
Message: Like it or not, go and tell! God's grace always shines! The destruction of Jerusalem was lamented in a despairing poem. After years of sinful behavior, Judah will be punished.

Messianic Prophecy: *"I will raise unto David a righteous branch"* (23:5–6; see also 30:9; 31:15; 33:15–16).

Ezekiel Portrays Jesus Christ, the Son of Man

FOCUS:
Message: Judgment to the rebellious and restoration for the obedient. Jesus is the wonderful four-faced man. The nation of Israel will be restored. The vision of the valley of the dry bones (37).

Holy Spirit Reference: 3:14; 11:1, 19; 18:31; 36:26

Messianic Prophecy: 34:23, 24, 29; 37:24–25

Daniel Portrays Jesus Christ, the Smiting Stone

FOCUS:
Message: This book describes the homecoming to the Sovereign God. Daniel is blessed for being faithful to God in a challenging situation. The book aids understanding of Bible prophecy, especially Revelation

Messianic Prophecy: The fourth Man in the fiery furnace (3:25); 7:14, 22.

FAMOUS BIBLE STORIES: Nebuchadnezzar's dream (2); Jews delivered from the fiery furnace (3:8–30); Daniel in the Lion's Den (6:10–28).

Chapter 2

Hosea Portrays Jesus Christ, Backslider Healer

FOCUS:
Message: Come back to God! is the call for repentance in this book. The prophet's marriage to the prostitute Gomer reflects God's relationship to Israel. "The Lord said to Hosea, Go, take unto thee a wife of whoredoms… for the land hath committed great whoredom, departing from the Lord" (1:2). Jesus is the faithful husband forever married to the backslider.

Messianic Prophecy: 3:5; 11:1

Joel Portrays Jesus Christ, Restorer and Baptizer

FOCUS:
Message: Repent, for "the day of the Lord is near." A plague of locusts depicts God's judgment on His disobedient, sinful people.

Amos Portrays Jesus Christ, Heavenly Husbandman

FOCUS:
Message: Call to Repentance! Prepare to meet your God! Real religion isn't just a ritual but treating people with justice. He calls for the restoration of Israel.

Obadiah Portrays Jesus Christ, Our Savior

FOCUS:
Message: Mount Zion Deliverance! Edom will suffer. Saviors shall come up on Mount Zion to judge, and the kingdom shall be the Lord's.

Jonah Portrays Jesus Christ, Resurrection and Life

FOCUS:

Message: Get up and go tell! Jonah was sent to preach of God's mercy and forgiveness, but he decided to flee his assignment. A reluctant prophet, running from God, Jonah was swallowed by a giant fish. He was in its belly three days, which is symbolic of the Saviors' stay in the tomb. God tests unrepentant Jonah. The book ends with a question.

Micah Portrays Jesus Christ, Witness against Rebellious Nations

FOCUS:

Message: Listen to God! Judah and Israel never learned their lessons. The people wavered between faith and apostasy, suffered many crises, and suffered for their idolatry.

Messianic Prophecy: "Out of thee shall He come forth unto me that is to be ruler in Israel" (5:1-2).

Nahum Portrays Jesus Christ, a Stronghold in the Day of Trouble

FOCUS:

Message: Look out, the Lord retaliates! Grievous, wicked Nineveh will fall before God's judgment. The book ends with a question.

Habakkuk Portrays Jesus Christ, the God of My Salvation

FOCUS:

Message: The just shall live by faith! When God appears to be unfair or unresponsive, trust him anyway.

Chapter 2

Exalt in God's goodness despite our imperfect understanding (3:16-19).

Zephaniah Portrays Jesus Christ, a Jealous God

FOCUS:
Message: Seek the Lord alone. Trust in the Lord because the day of the Lord is imminent with heavy judgment.

Haggai Portrays Jesus Christ, the Desire of All Nations

FOCUS:
Message: Rebuild the temple. Jews were persuaded to glorify God by rebuilding His treasury-supported temple.

Messianic Prophecy: "I will shake all nations, and the desire of all nations shall come" (2:7).

Zechariah Portrays Jesus Christ, Righteous Branch

FOCUS:
Message: Covenant Relationship. Jewish exiles should rebuild their temple, but God wanted more. He wanted a restored relationship. The book tells of Christ's first and second coming.

Messianic Prophecy: "I will bring forth my servant the Branch" (3:8). See also: 10:9-10; 11:12-13; 12:10; 13:1, 6-7; 14:4, 9.

Malachi Portrays Jesus Christ, Son of Righteousness

FOCUS:
Message: Indictment, Instruction, Judgment and Hope. This book foretells the coming of John the Baptist

and Jesus. We have a great, loving, and holy God, who has unchanging and glorious purposes for His people.

Messianic Prophecy: 3:1–3; 4:2

Chapter 2

Initially, Sarah could not conceive. Because social custom demanded it, Sarah urged her husband to have an affair. The primary purpose of marriage was to have children. If a wife was sterile, it was her responsibility to give one of her maids to her husband, so the family name could be continued. Sarah was simply doing her duty per the culture of that time. In fact, an ancient legal system, the Code of Hammurabi, spelled out the procedures for Sarah's actions.

God intended to create a line of descendants through the child of promise, Isaac. After Sarah birthed Isaac, she banished Hagar and Ishmael, whose birth was not divinely sanctioned. But God provided for them. God told distressed Abraham, "I will make the son of the maidservant into a nation also, because he is your offspring" (Genesis 21:13). The "familial" wars are still raging.

From Adam to the present time, sin brings discord to the family of God. Adam and Eve sinned, and in the next chapter, Cain kills Abel. Joseph's half-brothers were jealous and hated him, so they sold him into slavery. But he fared well because the Word stated repeatedly "God was with him." David's sin with Bathsheba and his sin afterward ("Thou shalt not kill. Thou shalt not commit adultery." Ex. 20:13-14) brought the sentence of death on their first born, and Nathan declared God's judgment that "the sword shall never depart from thine house... I will raise up evil against thee out of thine own house...."

In the very next chapter, his daughter Tamar is raped by her half-brother Amnon, who was later killed by her full brother Absalom. David suffered! Families are suffering for breaking the commandments. Sex outside marriage is the only sin that is committed against one's own body (I Corinthians 6:18). What is the reason for suffering? The Father is not pleased. Unbiblical actions discredit (blaspheme) the Word of God (Titus 2:5; II Samuel 12:14). Watch the patterns!

All of humanity is flawed, under the penalty of spiritual death, and in need of a savior because of sin in the Garden of Eden. Christians who are saved chose Jesus Christ as the *Way* back to spiritual union with God the Father for life in the spirit. The way we can live forever spiritually is to know the *Truth*, and we then have the life everlasting! The new commandment is *love* (John 13:34). *"God is love"* (I John 4:16). *"Jesus said, "I am the way, the truth and the life; no man comes to the Father, but by me"* (John 14:6).

Love and obedience are rewarded. Through conversation and demonstration, help prepare children to follow the Lord on the road ahead. Tell the next generation the praiseworthy deeds of the Lord, His power, and the wonders he has done. Teach our children and our children's children about God and His commandments so that future generations will love and worship Him. Our homes will be sanctified and blessed. Read Psalm 78:1–8 and Deuteronomy 11:18–32

May I suggest where to start Bible study with children? There are thirty-one days in most months, and thirty-one chapters in Proverbs. For wisdom, read a chapter a day to keep ignorance away. Read the date that corresponds with the chapter number. Have a pencil in hand to underline the verse that blesses you most. If a day is missed, focus on the current date. Repeat monthly until the Holy Spirit provides guidance to other books of the Bible.

Chapter 2

The New Testament

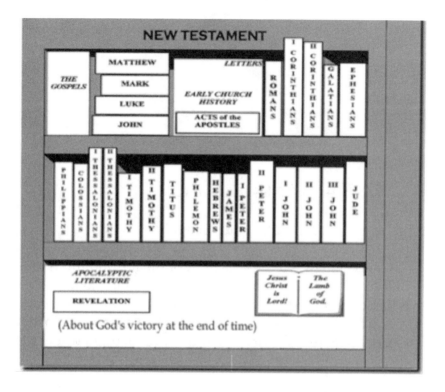

The Bible Explained

JESUS
The Lamb of God

The Four Gospels

The Gospels tell the *good news* of the life and ministry of Jesus Christ. They portray God in flesh and blood, who is Savior and Lord, the ultimate sacrifice. No more animal sacrifices are necessary. Jesus is the Lamb of God! Each Gospel tells Jesus' story from four points of view. Each disciple emphasizes our Savior differently, yet tells the same story.

Since man was spiritually separated from God

> Because of Adam's sin,
> God became like us
> To bring us back to Him!

The only person who can serve as a mediator between God and man is the One who *is* both God and man. "In the beginning was the Word and the Word was with God, and the *Word Was God*" (John 1:1).

Chapter 2

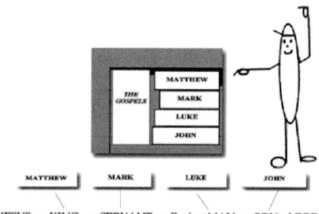

JESUS, as KING, as SERVANT, as Perfect MAN, as SON of GOD

Matthew Portrays Jesus Christ, Our Messiah

FOCUS:

Jesus fulfils the Old Testament prophecies of a coming messiah. The hinge of history (*His Story*) is found on the door of a Bethlehem stable.

FAMOUS STORIES: Visit of Magi (2:1-12), Baptism of Jesus and Escape to Egypt (3:13-17), Little Children and Jesus (19:13-15), the Lord's Supper (26:17-29), Jesus Prays at Gethsemane (26:36-46), Jesus on Trial (27:1-26), The Crucifixion — Jesus' *blood* shed for our sins (27:31-56), Burial of Jesus (27:31-56), The Resurrection (28:1-15)

Miracles: Healing the Centurion's Servant (8:5-13), Curing Man with Leprosy (8:1-4), Calming the Sea (8:23-27), Healing Child with a Demon (17:14-21), Jesus Walks on Water (14:22-33), Healing Woman (9:18-26), Healing Man (12:9-13), Divorce and Christians (5:32) Feeding the 5,000 (14:14-21), Finding Money for Taxes (17:24-27)

Parables: The Sower (13:3-32), Mustard Seed (13:31-32), House Built on a Rock (7:24-27), Lost Sheep (18:12-14), Laborers in the Vineyard (20:1-16)

Mark Portrays Jesus Christ, the Servant of God

FOCUS:
Jesus is God's Son, a suffering servant and sacrifice who came to die.

Famous Stories: Baptism of Jesus (1:9-11), Jesus Heals Many (1:21-34), Jesus Walks on Water (6:45-52), Little Children and Jesus (10:13-16), Jesus Clears the Temple (11:15-18), The Lord's Supper (14:12-25), Jesus on Trial (14:53-65), The Crucifixion—His blood shed for our sin (15:20-41), The Burial of Jesus (15:42-47), The Resurrection (16:1-8), Appears to His Disciples (16:14)

Miracles: Healing Blind Bartimaeus (10:46-52), Fig Tree Curse (11:12-14)

Parables: The Sower (4:2-20), Mustard Seed (4:30-32)

Luke Portrays Jesus Christ, the Son of Man

FOCUS:
Jesus is the Savior of all people, whether Jew or Gentile. "To inherit eternal life?... Thou shalt love the Lord thy God with all thy heart, and... love thy neighbor as thyself." (10:25, 27) The first part of this NT love commandment covers the first four of the Old Testament Ten commandments; the second part covers the last six.

FAMOUS STORIES: Birth of Jesus (2:1-20), The Boy Jesus at the Temple (2:41-52), The Baptism of Jesus (3:21-23), Jesus Tempted by Satan (4:1-13), Jesus talks to

Chapter 2

Zacchaeus (19:1-10), The Lord's Supper (22:7-38), Jesus is Arrested (22:47-53), Crucifixion—blood shed for our sin (23:26-49), Resurrection (24:1-12)

Miracles: Restoring the Crippled Woman (13:10-17), Miraculous Fish Catch (5:1-11), Raising a Widow's Son (7:11-15), Healing a man with dropsy (14:1-6), Cleansing Ten Lepers (17:11-19) Good Samaritan: (10:25-37), Rich Fool (12:16-21), Prodigal Son (15:11-32), Rich Man and Lazarus (16:10-31), Pharisee and Publican (18:10-14), Unjust Steward (16:1-9)

Parables: The Sower (8:4-15), Mustard Seed (13:18-19), House Built upon a Rock (6:46-49), Lost Sheep (15:3-7), Good Samaritan (10:25-37), Rich Fool (12:16-21), Prodigal Son (15:11-32), Rich Man and Lazarus (16:10-31), Pharisee and Publican (18:10-14), Unjust Steward (16:1-9)

John Portrays Jesus Christ, the Son of God.

FOCUS:
The only Savior of the world is Jesus, God in the flesh. John recognized the Lamb! By believing Jesus is the Christ, you may have life in his name. John provides more extensive treatments of Jesus' reasons for coming to earth than the other three Gospels.

FAMOUS STORIES: Jesus Teaches Nicodemus, the Teacher (3:1-21), Jesus on Trial (18:28-19:16), The Resurrection (20:1-18), Jesus Appears to Disciples (20:19-31)

Miracles: Turning water to wine (2:1-11), Restoring sight to a blind man (9:1-41), Raising Lazarus from the dead (11:1-44), "Jesus wept" (11:35) Jesus was groaning, troubled that the mourners did not know He had the power to do all things.

Parables: Many in John are the same as in the other three Gospels.

FAMOUS VERSES: "In the beginning was the Word and the Word was with God, and the Word was God" (1:1). "And the Word was made flesh and dwelt among us" (1:14). Told to Nicodemus, the teacher: "That which is born of the flesh is flesh; and that which is born of the Spirit is spirit... you must be born again" (3:5-7).

MOST FAMOUS VERSE IN THE BIBLE:

"For God so loved the world, that He gave His only begotten Son, that whosoever believeth in him should not perish, but have everlasting life" (3:16).

Early Church History

After Jesus' ascension, do you want to know what the disciples did? They did the *acts* of the Apostles! The book of Acts describes the outpouring of the Holy Spirit on the Church at Pentecost. The first twelve chapters focus on the apostle *Peter* as the central figure. Chapters 13-28 focus on Paul, the former tyrant Saul.

Chapter 2

Acts is:
Written by Luke;
Covers a period of approximately thirty-three years; and
Covers a period from Christ's ascension to Paul's imprisonment.

Jesus spoke just before He ascended, "But you shall receive power, when the Holy Spirit has come upon you; and you shall be witnesses to Me in Jerusalem, and to the end of the earth" (Acts 1:8). Renewal and spiritual regeneration were what happened when "divided tongues, as of fire, filled all with the Holy Spirit... the Spirit gave them utterance" (Acts 2:1-4).

Acts Portrays Jesus Christ, the Living Lord

FOCUS:
The Holy Spirit's arrival heralds the beginning of the Christian church. The Acts of the Apostles describes how Jesus' followers responded after His ascension to heaven when they were filled with the Holy Spirit.

FAMOUS STORIES: Jesus Taken Up to Heaven (1:1-11), Day of Pentecost—Apostles filled with the Holy Ghost given the ability to speak in other languages (tongues) (2:1-13), Peter's Sermon (2:14-47), Peter Heals Crippled Beggar (3:1-10), Stephen's Sermon (7) followed by Stephen's stoning (7:51-60), Saul's Conversion (Paul became his name after conversion.) (9:1-19), Paul and Silas in Prison (16:16-40), The Shipwreck (27:1-28:10)

Imprisonment did not stop Paul from preaching. To the churches where he had preached, he wrote *letters!* He had preached to churches in many places, so he wrote letters to those churches and pastors. He preached how the family works best, by respecting God's Genesis 3 punishment.

The Bible Explained

He advocated moral integrity and forgiveness in most letters, and love, the new commandment in all.

When you hear the suffix -*ans*, the letter is to a special group, whether He had been there or not. (Paul never met the congregation in Rome.) For example, to the church in Rome, he wrote to the Romans, the church in Corinth, Corinthians; Ephesus, Ephesians; Thessalonica, Thessalonians; Philippi, Philippians, and so forth.

LETTERS

Jesus Christ's Truth to the Church and Pastors

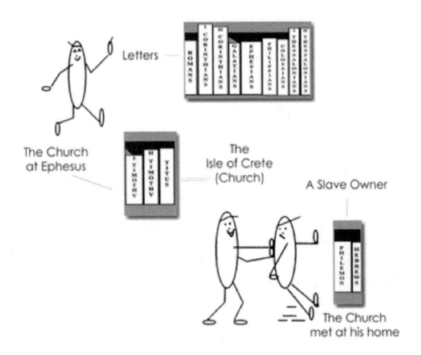

Chapter 2

Romans Portrays Jesus Christ, Our Righteousness

FOCUS:
Romans is called a theology book for its thorough explanation of the Christian faith. Sinners are saved by faith through grace, which justifies, bringing about reformation. This book is a theology textbook and a turning point for many.

FAMOUS VERSES: "All have sinned, and come short of the glory of God" (3:32). "Therefore being justified by faith, we have peace with God through our Lord Jesus Christ" (5:1). "We know that all things work together for good to them that love God, to them who are the called according to his purpose" (8:28). We should "present our bodies a living sacrifice... which is your reasonable service. (... and spiritual worship). And be not conformed to this world; but be ye transformed by the renewing of your mind" (12:1–2).

I Corinthians Portrays Jesus Christ, the Rock

FOCUS:
Paul tackles sin problems in the church at Corinth. This book teaches on marriage, the Lord's Supper, spiritual gifts, and Christian liberty. It warns against filing lawsuits against Christians and against immoral relationships, giving straightforward advice. It is direct and practical, giving God's perspective on some hot topics. Paul includes uplifting words about love and the resurrection.

Important Chapters: Spiritual gifts (12), True agape love defined! (13)

FAMOUS VERSES: "Your body is the temple of the Holy Ghost which is in you" (6:19). We *are* the church! "The first man Adam was made a living soul; the last Adam was make a quickening spirit" (15:45). "The first man is of the earth, earthy: the second man is the Lord from heaven" (15:47). Our earthly condition is such that our Adamic bodies somehow must be changed. The body that bears the image of the man of dust (the first Adam) must inevitably be changed into the incorruption and immortality of the body that bears the image of the man from heaven (the second Adam). "And as we have borne the image of the earthy, we shall also bear the image of the heavenly" (15:49). The Resurrection of saved believers is explained: "for the trumpet shall sound, and the dead shall be raised incorruptible" (15:52).

II Corinthians Portrays Jesus Christ's Sufficiency

FOCUS:
Paul defends his ministry to the troubled Corinthian Church experiencing inner strife. Second Corinthians was written to calm disagreements, restore unity, and reestablish leadership. Troublemakers questioned Paul's authority, and he responded with practical conflict resolution.

FAMOUS VERSES: "For he hath made him to be sin for us, who knew no sin; that we might be made the righteousness of God in him" (5:21). Paul suffered a "thorn in the flesh" (12:7), which God refused to take away, telling him instead, "My grace is sufficient… for my strength is made perfect in weakness" (12:9).

Chapter 2

Galatians Portrays Jesus Christ, Our Liberty

FOCUS:
Christians are free from restrictive Jewish laws. Old Testament rules do not control Christians' lives, but God's Spirit should. Paul denounces false teaching in this book.

FAMOUS VERSES: "Walk in the Spirit, and you shall not fulfil the lust of the flesh. For the flesh lusteth against the Spirit, and the Spirit against the flesh: and these are contrary the one to the other: so that ye cannot do the things that ye would" (5:16–17). "The Fruit of the Spirit is love, joy, peace, longsuffering, gentleness, goodness, faith, meekness, temperance: against such there is no law" (5:22–23). "The just shall live by faith" (3:11). "Abraham had two sons... he who was of the bondwoman (Ishmael) was born after the flesh; but the son of the freewoman (Isaac) was by promise" (4:22–23).

Ephesians Portrays Jesus Christ, Our All in All

FOCUS:
Christians are all members of Jesus' "body," the church. We are instructed to put clothing on the fleshly visible body and to put Jesus Christ on the unseen, invisible spirit body.

IMPORTANT VERSES: "Put on the whole armor of God, that you may be able to stand against the wiles of the devil" (6:11). "In time past you walked according to the course of this world, according to the prince of the power of the air, the spirit that now worketh in the children of disobedience" (2:2). (All references to the devil/Satan) "Among whom also we all had conversation in time past in the lusts of our flesh, fulfilling the desires of the flesh and of the mind; and were by nature the children of wrath, even as others" (2:3).

NOTE: See Chapter 6, Spiritual Warfare Explained.

Marriage/Family Advice in accordance with punishment levied by God in Genesis 3 is given in this book. "Wives, submit yourselves unto your own husbands, as unto the Lord" (5:22). "Husbands, love your wives" (5:25). "Wife [should]... reverence (respect) her husband" (5:33). (Read and heed all of 5:21-33.) "Children, obey your parents in the Lord: for this is right. Honor thy Father and mother; (which is the first commandment with promise)" (6:1-2). "Fathers, provoke not your children to wrath: but bring them up in the nurture and admonition of the Lord" (6:4).

Philippians Portrays Jesus Christ, Our Joy

FOCUS:
This is a "friendship letter" between the apostle Paul and a beloved church of believers in the city of Philippi, showing *phileo* love! In it are multiple references to joy and rejoicing. It is a very upbeat letter of thanksgiving.

IMPORTANT VERSES: "Forgetting those things which are behind, and reaching forth unto those things which are before, I press toward the mark for the prize of the high calling of God in Christ Jesus" (3:13-14). Get Over It! Instead of things of a bad past, for the peace of God, focus on: "... whatsoever things are true... honest... just... pure... lovely... good report... virtue... praise, think on these things" (4:8).

Chapter 2

Colossians Portrays Jesus Christ, Our Life

FOCUS:
Jesus Christ is supreme over everyone and everything. Christ is preeminent in all, including love, the bond of perfection, and importance. Forgive and just get along!

IMPORTANT VERSES: Pray Colossians 1:9-12 for everyone, including those whom you love or like, and especially those whom you do not love or /like. Reword it to suit the person or situation and pray these verses for them in the name of Jesus.

Chapter 3 — Paul tells more about how to dress our spirit man in the Word. The words, "Put on..." are mentioned several times, and who we must allow to dwell in us is emphasized.

Family and Marriage: "Wives submit yourselves unto your own husbands... Husbands, Love your wives and be not bitter against them. Children, obey your parents... Father's provoke not your children to anger, lest they be discouraged" (4:18-20).

I Thessalonians Portrays Jesus Christ, the Coming One

FOCUS:
Jesus will return to gather His followers to Him. All are told we must live right at all times because Jesus is coming back.

IMPORTANT VERSES: "For the Lord himself shall descend from heaven with a shout, with the voice of the archangel, and with the trump of God; and the dead in Christ shall rise first; Then we which are alive and remain shall be caught up together with them in the clouds, to meet the Lord in the air: and so shall we ever be with the Lord" (5:13-18). Two of the shortest verses in the Bible are: "Rejoice evermore" (5:16) and "Pray without ceasing" (5:17).

II Thessalonians Portrays Jesus Christ, Our Returning Lord

FOCUS:
Christians should work until Jesus returns. This book provides an eternal perspective. Look forward to Jesus' return, stay busy doing good, and spread the Word.

IMPORTANT VERSES: "And then shall that Wicked be revealed, whom the Lord shall consume with the spirit of his mouth, and destroy with the brightness of his coming: Even him, whose coming is after the working of Satan with all power and signs and lying wonders... because they believed not the love of the truth, that they might be saved. And for this cause God shall send them a strong delusion, that they should believe a lie: that they all might be damned who believed not the truth, but had pleasure in unrighteousness" (2:8-12).

I Timothy Portrays Jesus Christ, Our Teacher

FOCUS:
Pastors are taught how to conduct their lives and churches. It summarizes guidelines for running a church and offers practical help to pastors and believers in their relationships with each other. Christian Admonition is given to bishops and deacons, who are to be *"the husband of one wife ruling their children and their own houses well"* (3:2, 12).

Chapter 2

IMPORTANT VERSES: "And without controversy great is the mystery of godliness: God was manifest in the flesh, justified in the Spirit, seen of angels, preached unto the Gentiles, believed on in the world, received up into glory" (3:16).

II Timothy Portrays Jesus Christ, Our Example

FOCUS:
The Apostle Paul's final words to a beloved coworker, giving warnings. Dying, he speaks of Jesus, the foundation of God, the hope of eternal life.

IMPORTANT VERSES: "In the last days' perilous times shall come, for men shall be lovers of their own selves... lovers of pleasures more than lovers of God,... from such turn away" (3:2–5). "For God hath not given us the spirit of fear; but of power, and of love, and of a sound mind" (1:7). "All Scripture is given by inspiration of God, and is profitable for doctrine, for reproof, for correction, for instruction in righteousness" (3:16).

Titus Portrays Jesus Christ, Our Pattern

FOCUS:
Church leaders are instructed how to live and teach because they are held to a high standard. The same pertains to the people in the pews, especially the elderly. He's told to refute false teachers, calm church disunity, and find quality leaders.

IMPORTANT VERSES: "A Bishop must be blameless, as the steward of God" (1:7). "The aged men [should] be sober, grave, temperate, sound in faith, in charity, in patience. The aged women... not given to much wine, teachers of good things;... teach the young women to be...

obedient to their own husbands, that the Word of God be not blasphemed. Young men… be sober minded" (2:5-6) so that "we should live soberly, righteously, and godly, in this present world; looking for that blessed hope, and glorious appearing of the great God and our Savior Jesus Christ" (2:12-13).

Philemon Portrays Jesus Christ, Lord and Master

FOCUS:
Paul begs mercy for a runaway slave converted to Christianity. It is a plea for grace, a forgiveness case study, and it is about being confident in obedience.

IMPORTANT VERSES: "If he hath wronged thee… put that on mine account… I will repay it:… thou owest me even thine own self besides" (1:18-19). "Having confidence in thy obedience I wrote unto thee, knowing that thou wilt also do more than I say" (1:21).
The Gospels—Matthew, Mark, Luke, and John tell of Jesus ministry on earth; whereas, *Hebrews* describes Jesus Christ's ministry in heaven, sitting at the right hand of God the Father, making intercession for us.

Hebrews Portrays Jesus Christ, Our Intercessor at the Throne

FOCUS:
Hebrews is sometimes called the fifth Gospel. Its author, who is unknown, urges followers to never quit. Jesus is better than any Old Testament person or sacrifice.

IMPORTANT CHAPTER: Hebrews 11 is called the Faith Hall of Fame.

Chapter 2

IMPORTANT VERSES: "Faith is the substance of things hoped for, the evidence of things not seen" (11:1). "He is able also to save them to the uttermost that come unto God by him, seeing he ever liveth to make intercession for them" (7:25). "The word of God is quick, and powerful, and sharper than any two-edged sword, piercing even to the dividing asunder of soul and spirit, and of the joints and marrow, and is a discerner of the thoughts and intents of the heart" (5:12). "Not forsaking the assembling of ourselves together, as the manner of some is, but exhorting one another: and so much the more, as ye see the day approaching" (10:25). " Let brotherly love continue. Be not forgetful to entertain strangers: for thereby some have entertained angels unawares" (13:1-2).

The General Letters

The general letters were authored by the names that appear on each book and were not directed to anyone in particular.

James Portrays Jesus Christ, Our Pattern

FOCUS:
Real Christian faith is shown by one's good works. Do you want wisdom? Ask God! James teaches that true faith

works. Trials produce opportunities for growth. A friend of the world is the enemy of God, who resists the proud and gives grace to the humble. James warns believers of bad habits and includes no-nonsense approach to hypocrisy. The final verses, 5:12–18, emphasize the importance of prayer.

IMPORTANT VERSES: "For as the body without the spirit is dead, so faith without works is dead also." (2:26) "The tongue is a fire, a world of iniquity: so is the tongue among our members, that it defileth the whole body, and setteth on fire the course of nature; and it is set on fire of hell." (3:6) "Therefore to him that knoweth to do good, and doeth it not, to him it is sin:" (4:17)

I Peter Portrays Jesus Christ, Precious Cornerstone of Our Faith

FOCUS:
A letter of comfort and encouragement to Christians. Suffering for the sake of Jesus is noble and good. Just shut up and *be* it, so others can *see* it, then they'll *believe* it! Peter writes about the reason for hope in the face of trouble and suffering.

IMPORTANT VERSES: "To whom coming, as unto a living stone, disallowed indeed of men, but chosen of God, and precious, ye also, as lively stones, are built up a spiritual house, an holy priesthood, to offer up spiritual sacrifices, acceptable to God by Jesus Christ" (2:4–5). "But ye are a chosen generation, a royal priesthood, and holy nation, a peculiar people; that ye should shew forth the praises of him who hath called you out of darkness into his marvelous light" (2:9). "Wives, be in subjection to your own husbands; that, if any obey not the word, they also may, without the word be won by the conversation of the wives" (3:1). "Holy women… being in subjection unto their own husbands: husbands, dwell with them according to knowledge, giving honor unto the wife, as unto the weaker vessel, as being heirs together of the grace of life; that your prays be not hindered" (3:5, 7).

II Peter Portrays Jesus Christ, Our Strength

FOCUS:
Peter warns against the dangers of false prophets and false teaching within the church. Beware of false teachers who bring damnable deviations, denying Jesus as Lord. Peter knew his death was near.

IMPORTANT VERSES: "Shortly I must put off this tabernacle, even as our Lord Jesus Christ hath shewed me" (1:14). "Beware lest ye also, being led away with the error of the wicked, fall from your own steadfastness" (3:17).

I John Portrays Jesus Christ, Our Life

FOCUS:
Jesus was a real man just as He is the real God. First John was written to combat denial of Christ's full deity and humanity. Without the light of Jesus, we would be in the dark about God. In John's book, we can find out more about the love of God.

IMPORTANT VERSES: "If any man sin, we have an advocate with the Father, Jesus Christ the righteous: and he is the propitiation for our sins: and not for ours only, but also for the sins of the whole world" (2:1-2). "Little children, it is the last time: and as ye have heard that antichrist shall come, even now are there many antichrists; whereby we know that it is the last time" (2:18). "Who is a liar but he that denieth that Jesus is the Christ? He is antichrist, that denieth the Father and the Son" (2:22). "Hereby perceive we the love of God, because he laid down his life for us:" (3:16) "For there are three that bear record in heaven, the Father, the Word, and the Holy Ghost: and these three are one" (5:7).

II John Portrays Jesus Christ, the Truth

FOCUS:
Beware of false teachers who deny Jesus' physical life on earth. Keep on target spiritually. This book also warns against any compromise with doctrinal error.

III John Portrays Jesus Christ, the Way

FOCUS:
Church leaders must be humble, not proud. If you've ever faced conflict in the church, while church fights may be unavoidable, this book teaches the way to handle them. The book also warns against refusing fellowship with true believers.

Jude Portrays Jesus Christ, Our Keeper

FOCUS:
Beware of heretical teachers and their dangerous doctrines. Jude gives a warning against false teachers and false doctrine. Ignoring spiritual warnings can be very perilous to health. Jude wrote to believers to urge them to contend for the faith (v. 3). Jude has a powerful impact and colorful imagery.
Before you read the book of Revelation, you may think, who is Jesus? Revelation answers that question profoundly! He is the righteous Judge coming to bring all things under his rule and power.

Chapter 2

And I saw the heavens open, and a white horse, and he who was sitting on it was called Faithful and True, and in righteousness He makes judgement and war. (19) His clothing is a robe dipped in **blood**, and the name in which He is called is The Word of God. On His robe and on His thigh He has the name written, "King of Kings" and "Lord of Lords."

That's the Sovereign God!

Revelation

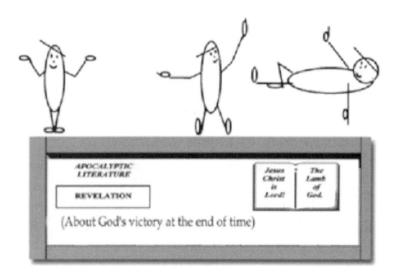

Revelation Portrays Jesus Christ, Our Triumphant King

FOCUS:
The book of Revelation was written by the Apostle John while exiled to the Isle of Patmos. The Tree of Life is described there. This book of prophecy amplifies the Old Testament book of Daniel. The Lamb is revealed in

heaven as the One who can open the seals. The Lord speaks His own words to John. God will judge evil and reward His saints. The book includes God's preview of coming attractions and the new and improved world we will enjoy forever. We win! The curse of sin will be gone, we'll live in perfect fellowship with the Lord Himself, and we will "reign for ever and ever" (22:5).

Jesus writes letters to seven churches, ending each with, "He that hath an ear, let him hear what the Spirit saith unto the churches" (2:11, 17, 29; 2:6, 13, 22). We all have physical ears, but not everyone has *spiritual* ears. Our bodies are "temples of the Holy Ghost" (the Holy Spirit; I Corinthians 6:19). We are each a Church, and God is speaking to you and me. Those of us who know Jesus Christ as Lord have spiritual ears. We hear!

IMPORTANT VERSES: The important verses of this book are too numerous to count, so you should read the entire book for yourself! However, please know: "And if any man shall take away from the words of the book of prophecy, God will take away his part out of the book of life, and out of the holy city, and from the things which are written in this book. He which testifieth these things saith, Surely I come quickly. Amen. Even so, come, Lord Jesus. The grace of our Lord Jesus Christ be with you all. AMEN" (22:19-21).

Chapter 2

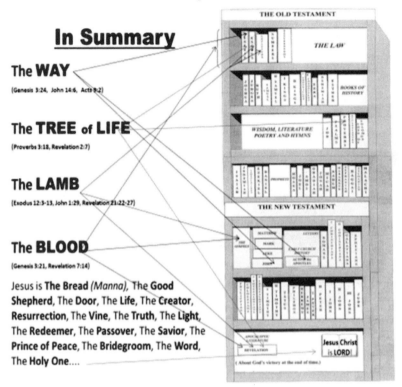

The Way: God drove man out of the garden to guard *the way* to the *tree of life*. (Genesis 3:24). Jesus said "I am *the way*..." (John 14:6). Followers of Jesus were called people of *the Way* (Acts 9:2).

The Tree of Life: Wisdom is called *the tree of life* (Proverbs 3:18). Conquerors will eat from the *tree of life* (Revelation 2:7).

The Lamb: The sacrifice for disobedience was a *lamb* (Exodus 12:3-13). John immediately recognized Jesus as *the Lamb* of God (John 1:29). No sun is needed because the presence and glory of God pervades the entire community in the new heaven and new earth. Its lamp is *the Lamb* (Revelation 21 22-27).

The Blood: *Blood* was shed for sin throughout the Pentateuch. Jesus shed blood as the final *blood* sacrifice for sin when He died on the cross. The *blood* of *the Lamb* of God cleanses from sin (Revelation 7:14).

These titles are all over the Bible. Keep reading the Word. The Holy Spirit will reveal His presence more!

Chapter 3

BIBLICAL NUMBERS EXPLAINED

One GOD

There is one body, and one Spirit, even as you are called in one hope of your calling; One Lord, one faith, one baptism, one God and Father of all, who is above all, And through all and in you all. (Ephesians 4:4–6)

The Bible Explained

Numerical Symbolism in the Bible

The Bible is filled with the Truths of The Word,
And we're constantly amazed by the order of God. Like
a tapestry, woven, gold strands fine as hair,
Pull a thread at one end and it wrinkles elsewhere.

One speaks of unity and *One* is God's name.
Two, the witness number,
Jesus the Faithful witness came.
Second person of the Godhead,
our flesh and blood example,
Two testaments to the Bible, both witnesses ample.
Three is God's number, Trinity, three in one,
We're baptized in the name of the Father,
Holy Spirit and Son.
The earth number is *four*,
The *four* corners of the world.
From the north, south, east and west the winds are unfurled.
Forty the number of testing,
the number 40 mentioned much.
Five the number of completeness,
senses, Pentateuch, toes and such.
On the *sixth* day God made MAN.
Six, the number of humanity.
Six hundred three score and six – Beast's number,
man's attempt at divinity.
The *perfect* number *seven*,
the day God rested from His plan,
Seven notes to the scale, 70 x 7 forgiveness,
70-year life span.
Eight starts new beginnings like an octave to a scale,
Circumcision, new birth, Jesus' transfiguration all tell.

Chapter 3

Ten, the number of fullness, Ten Commandments to the law, the number of plagues on Egypt, the tribulation, downfall.
God's governmental earth number twelve,
4 x 3 judges all,
(The nine and eleven are more difficult to call)
There were *twelve* apostles Jesus picked to "Go Tell," *Twelve* patriarchs, *twelve* thrones judging the *twelve* tribes of Israel.

As you read The Word and become more aware of God's order of numbers that you see appear there,
Give God the praise, all who are living
the life of the Son as you worship with thanksgiving.

The Symbolism of Numbers Scripture Text
(Partial List)

One Deuteronomy 6:4; Zechariah 14:9; Ephesians 4 : 4 – 6
Two John 8:17; Revelation 1:5; 11:3
Three Matthew 28:19; I Thessalonians 5:23
Four Isaiah 11:12; Ezekiel 7:2; Revelation 4:6; 7:1; 20:8
Five Matthew 14:19
Six Revelation 13:18
Seven Matthew 18:22; Psalm 90:10
Eight Genesis 17:12
Ten Exodus 34:28; Revelation 2:10
Twelve Matthew 19:28; Revelation 4:4; 21:16

The Bible portrays Jesus Christ as the Savior of the World

A Few More Interesting Facts

The Bible contains sixty-six books, attributed to forty authors, covering a period of approximately 1600 years.

The word *Bible* comes from the Greek word *biblios.*

The word *testament* means "covenant," or agreement; the Old Testament is about man's salvation before Christ; it is the law. The New Testament is about man's salvation after Christ came — grace.

From Adam to Abraham, we have the history of the human race.

From Abraham to Christ, we have the history of the chosen race.

From Christ on, we have the history of the church.

The meaning of God, man, sin, redemption, justification, sanctification, glorification: in two words — grace and glory and in one word — Jesus.

   The book of Hebrews quotes the Old Testament (quotations or allusions) eighty-five times.

 Biblical Numbers

The message of the Bible is the message of Jesus Christ who said, "I am the way, the truth and the life."

It's the story of salvation, the story of our redemption; Numbers will help you concentrate and keep attention.

Chapter 3

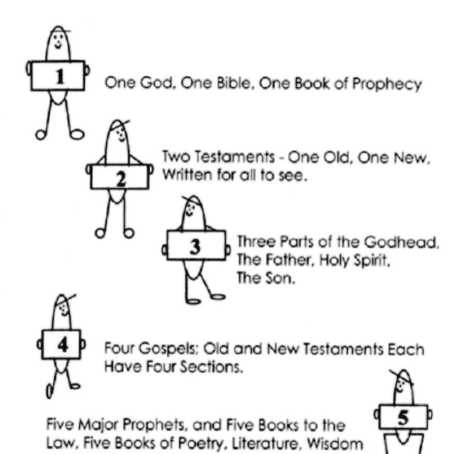

The Bible Explained

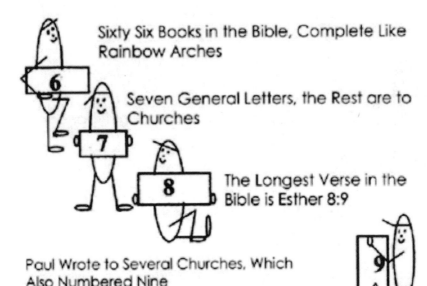

Sixty Six Books in the Bible, Complete Like Rainbow Arches

Seven General Letters, the Rest are to Churches

The Longest Verse in the Bible is Esther 8:9

Paul Wrote to Several Churches, Which Also Numbered Nine

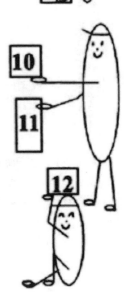

There are Ten Commandments God Gave Moses in the Law

Eleven Letters written to Churches, Attributed to Apostle Paul

Twelve Minor Prophets, Twelve History Books Recall

Chapter 3

How God in flesh did live a life of divine perfection?
So man could get to God, whose Word contains direction.

God incarnate is the Word, the author of Creation
To offer each and every man *eternal salvation*!

Three "Tree of Life" Lines

Mankind Was Banished From Paradise to Protect Us From Living in Our Sinful State Forever.

"So (God) drove out the man; and He placed at the east of the garden of Eden the cherubim and a flaming sword which turned every way, to keep *and* guard the way to the *tree of life.*" (Genesis 3:24 Amplified)

Gain Access to the Tree of Life By Choosing to Find Wisdom in the Word.

"Happy (blessed, fortunate, enviable) is the man who finds skillful and godly Wisdom, and the man who gets understanding [drawing it forth from God's Word and life's experiences]. For the gaining of it is better than the gaining of silver and the profit of it better than find gold. Skillful *and* godly Wisdom is more precious than rubies: and nothing you can wish for is to be compared to her. Length of days is in her right hand, and in her left hand are riches and honor. Her ways are highways of pleasantness, and all her paths are peace. She is a *tree of life* to those who lay hold on her; and happy (blessed, fortunate, to be envied) is anyone who holds her fast" (Proverbs 3:13-18 Amplified)

Overcome to Eat From the Tree of Life

"He who is able to hear, let him listen to and give heed to what the Spirit says to the assemblies (churches). To him who overcomes (is victorious), I will grant to eat [of the fruit] of the *tree of life*, which is in the paradise of God." (Revelation 2:7 Amplified)

"O taste and see that the Lord is good! Blessed is the man who trusts and takes refuge in Him." (Psalm 34:8 Amplified)

Chapter 4

BIBLICAL TRINITY EXPLAINED

Jesus Christ Is God

For in Him dwells all the fullness of the Godhead bodily. (Colossians 2:9)

The Bible Explained

What Does the Bible Say?

If we take the very first words of the very first verse of the first chapter of the first book of the Bible, we see the Trinity. What does it say? It says, "In the beginning God created..." Those are actually three Hebrew words: *berashith*, "in the beginning"; *bahrah*, "He created"; Gods (notice that is plural), *Elohim*. The singular for God is *El*, and the plural is *Elohim*. What it is saying is "In the beginning, Gods [plural], He created."

That is not very good grammar... or is it? It is if you happen to be God because there you see the tri-unity of God, three in one.

"For in Him dwells all the
fullness of the Godhead bodily"
(Colossians 2:9)

And the LORD shall be King over all the earth.
In that day it shall be —

"The LORD is One,"
And

His Name One
(Zechariah 14:9)

Chapter 4

Understanding the Trinity

There is a trinity that threatens our society.

The world is the external foe.
The flesh is the internal foe.
The devil is the infernal foe.
The world provides the match, the flesh provides the gasoline, and the devil strikes the match.

Matthew 4:1-11 tells how the devil tempted Jesus. Jesus answered each time, "... *it is written.*" Like our Savior, we must also use the sword of the Spirit, which is the Word of God to fight our battles when the schemes of the devil work to deceive us.

Ephesians 2:1-3 names the unholy trinity best:

> "And you He made alive, who were dead in trespasses and sins, in which you once walked according to he course of this world, following the prince of the power of the air, the spirit that is now at work in the sons of disobedience. Among these we all once lived in the passions of our flesh, following the desires of body and mind, and so we were by nature children of wrath, like the rest of mankind." Ephesians 2:1-3

Read all of Ephesians 2 to further understand the grace of salvation through Christ Jesus, our God of grace.

And you are complete in Him, who is the
head of all principality and power.
(Colossians 2:10)

Now may...God...sanctify you completely; and may your
whole spirit, and soul and body be preserved blameless
at the coming of our Lord Jesus Christ.
(I Thessalonians 5:23)

Let this mind be in you which was also in Christ Jesus, who,
being in the form of God...taking the form of a bondservant,
and coming in the likeness of men.
(Philippians 2:5-7)

"...If any man will come after me, let him deny himself,
and take up his cross daily, and follow me."
(Luke 9:23)

Chapter 4

Dress your body ("the temple of God") in clothing. Dress your spirit and soul in "invisible" armor, the Whole Armor of God, Jesus Christ.

The Glory of The Triune God
Holy, Holy, Holy! Lord God Almighty

Holy, Holy, Holy, Lord God Almighty!
Early in the morning our song shall rise to Thee.
Holy, Holy, Holy! Merciful and Mighty,
God in Three Persons, blessed Trinity!

Holy, Holy, Holy! All the saints adore Thee.
Casting down their golden crowns around the glassy sea;
Cherubim and seraphim falling down before Thee,
Which wert, and art, and evermore shalt be.

Holy, Holy, Holy! Though the darkness hide Thee
Though the eye of sinful man Thy glory may not see.
Only Thou art Holy; there is none beside Thee.
Perfect in power, in love and purity.

Holy, Holy, Holy! Lord God Almighty!
All Thy works shall praise Thy name, in earth and sky and sea.
Holy, Holy, Holy! Merciful and Mighty.
God in Three Persons, blessed Trinity.

WORDS: Reginald Heber, 1826 *(Revelation 4:8-11)*
MUSIC: John B. Dykes, 1861

This classic Christian hymn proclaims the glory of the Triune God best. It would be most appropriate for this song to be the opening hymn at Christian Churches worldwide.

This classic Christian hymn proclaims the glory of the Triune God best. Read all the words as you sing the song.

The Bible Explained

HOLY, HOLY, HOLY! LORD GOD ALMIGHTY

> And they do not rest day or night, saying: "Holy, Holy, Holy, Lord God Almighty, who was and is and is to come!"
> (Revelation 4:8)

Reginald Heber was born April 21, 1783, to a minister and his wife in an English village. Following graduation from Oxford where he excelled in poetry, Heber succeeded his father as vicar in his family's parish.

He continued writing hymns for his own church and I was during the sixteen ears in the obscure parish of Hodnet that Heber wrote all 57 of his hymns, including the great missionary hymn, "From Greenland's Icy Mountains," which exhorted missionaries to take the gospel to faraway places.

At age 40 he was appointed to oversee the Church of England's ministries in India. Arriving in Calcutta, he set out on a 16-month tour of his diocese, visiting mission stations across India. While in the village of Trichinopoly on April 3, 1826, he preached to a large crowd in the hot sun and afterward, plunged into a pool of cool water. He suffered a stroke and drowned. It was after his death that his widow, finding his 57 hyms in a trunk, succeeded in publishing his hymns written and adapted to the weekly service of the church year. In this volume was the great Trinitarian hymn based on Revelation 4:8-11, "Holy, Holy, Holy, Lord God Almighty".

(Excerpts from "Then Sings My Soul" by Robert J. Morgan)

Chapter 4

Satan Mimics God

Watch and pray that you may not enter into temptation; the spirit indeed is willing, but the flesh is weak. (Matthew 26:41)

That which is born of the flesh is flesh; and that which is born of the Spirit is spirit... you must be born again. (John 3:6-7)

It is the Spirit that gives life; the flesh is of no avail (profits nothing): the words that I have spoken to you are spirit and life. (John 6:63)

Walk by the Spirit and do not gratify the desires of the flesh. For the desires of the flesh are against the Spirit, and the desires of the Spirit are against the flesh; for these are opposed to each other, to prevent you from doing what you would. (Galatians 5:16–17)

Read all of Galatians 5, especially verses 18–25 to see the works of the flesh. Those who live like that will not inherit the kingdom of God.

> For this cause I bow my knees unto the Father of our Lord, Jesus Christ, of whom the whole family in heaven and earth is named, that he would grant you… to be strengthened with might by His Spirit in the inner man; that Christ may dwell in your hearts by faith. (Ephesians 3:14–17)

Humanity (you & me)

It's downright *super*natural!

Chapter 4

There is therefore now no condemnation to them which are in Christ Jesus, who walk not after the flesh, but after the Spirit. For the law of the Spirit of life in Christ Jesus has made me free from the law of sin and death.

For what the law could not do, in that it was weak through the flesh, God sending his own Son in the likeness of sinful flesh, and for sin, condemned sin in the flesh: that the righteousness of the law might be fulfilled in us, who walk not after the flesh, but after the Spirit.

For they that are after the flesh do mind the things of the flesh; but they that are after the Spirit the things of the Spirit. For to be carnally minded is death; but to be spiritually minded is life and peace. Because the carnal mind is enmity against God: for t is not subject to the law of God, neither indeed can be. So then they that are in the flesh cannot please God. (Romans 8:1-8; see all of Romans 8.)

That which is born of the flesh is flesh; and that which is born of the Spirit is spirit. Marvel not that I said to you, you must be born again. (John 3:6-7. See all of John 3:1-21 and Galatians 5:22-25)

Four Greek Words for Love

- *Agape*   charity, the love of God. (1 Corinthians 13:4-8)
- *Eros*   sexual passion, intimate, physical
- *Phileo*   friendship, brotherly love, warm feeling
- *Storge*   family love, natural between parents and children, love for one's country, favorite team, etc.

The Bible Explained

GOD'S SUPERNATURAL DNA IS ALL OVER CREATION!

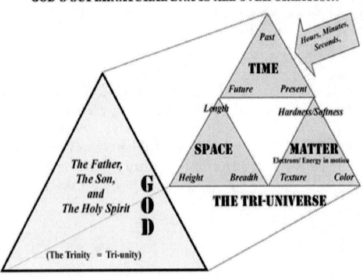

THE SOLAR SYSTEM = 9 PLANETS (3 × 3)

Chapter 4

Redemption in Christ

Salvation by Grace Through Faith in Christ,...Renewed in the Spirit,...One Church, Many Parts,...

Dress your body ("the temple of God") in clothing, Dress your spirit and soul in 'invisible' armor, The Whole Armor of God,...

"...You must be born again"

(Read all of John 3:1-13)

JESUS CHRIST

"...in the image of God He created him; male and female He created them."
(Genesis 1:26)

"...he that sows to his flesh will of the flesh reap corruption, but he who sows to the Spirit will of the Spirit reap everlasting life.
(Galatians 6:8)

"I am the vine, you are the branches: He that abides in Me, and I in him, the same brings forth much fruit: for without Me you can do nothing."
(John 15:5)

THE GREATEST - GOD'S MINIATURE BIBLE
(John 3:16 Outlined)

God – the greatest lover

so loved – the greatest degree

the world – the greatest company

that He gave – the greatest act

His only begotten Son – the greatest gift

that whoever believes – the greatest simplicity

in Him – the greatest person

should not perish – the greatest promise

but – the greatest difference

have – the greatest certainty

everlasting life – the greatest possession

The most famous Scripture verse in the Bible!

Chapter 5

CONFIRMATION

They Are One!

Jesus said, He who has seen me has seen the Father. (John 14:9)

He is the exact likeness of the unseen God (the visible representation of the invisible); He is the First born of all creation. (Colossians 1:15 Amplified version)

The Bible Explained

Now... get this!!!

God
the Father,

Jesus Christ
the Son,

and

The Holy Spirit
(aka The Holy Ghost)

are *one*!

"For there are three that bear witness in Heaven: The Father, the Word, and the Holy Spirit: and these three are One" (I John 5:7).

Chapter 5

Do You Believe in Water?

H_2O exists as a solid, a gas and as a liquid.

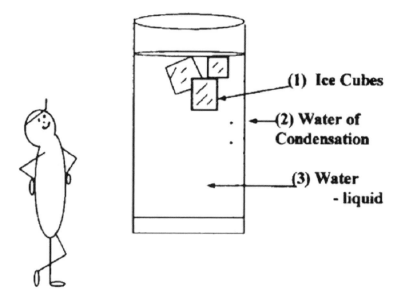

A glass of ice water contains H2O in all three forms at the same time.

The Bible Explained

Since you believe in this natural law, then by faith, believe in the supernatural.

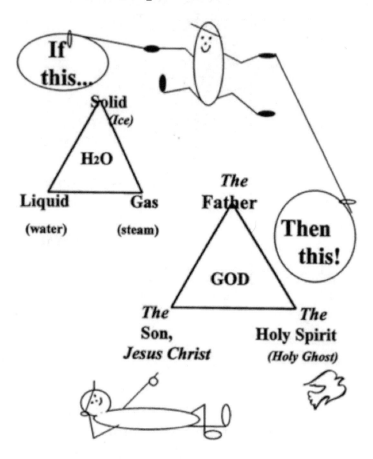

The Father gave the Son.
The Son gave the Spirit.
The Spirit gives us Life,
So we can give the gift of love.
(Read I Corinthians 13 — the Love Chapter.)

Chapter 5

Here is another example of the Trinity in the form of a pretzel.

For in Him (Christ) dwells all of the fullness of the Godhead bodily. (Colossians 2:9) O taste and see that the LORD is good: blessed is the man that trusts Him. (Psalm 34:8)

The Bible speaks of many mysteries.

And without controversy great is the mystery of Godliness: God was manifested in the flesh, justified in the Spirit, seen by angels, preached among the Gentiles, believed on in the world, received up into glory. (I Timothy 3:16)
By this you know the Spirit of God: Every spirit that confesses that Jesus Christ has come in the flesh is of God: And every spirit that does not confess that Jesus Christ has come in the flesh is not of God: And this is the spirit of the Antichrist, which you have heard was coming; and is now already in the world. (I John 4:2-3)

JESUS was 100 percent man (yet without sin); He became like us, so sinful man could touch the hand of God.

He was born to lost mankind (The Baby that Mary delivered; Matthew 2:6–23)

He said to His Mother "My hour is not yet come." (John 2:4–5)

He touched people to heal them (John 9:6–7; Matthew 8:3; Luke 22:51)

Jesus wept, groaned, and was troubled. (John 11:33, 35)

He submitted to water baptism (Matthew 3:16)

Jesus slept and grew weary. (John 4:6)

He walked on land. He said, "Come." (John 1:36, 39)

He thirsted. (John 19:28)

He questioned God. (Matthew 27:46)

He shed His blood. (Luke 22:20; John 19:34)

Jesus said, "Before Abraham was, I am." (John 8:58)

The Jews were angry because they knew the Name of God is "I AM." (Exodus 3:13–14)

A prophet who wasn't accepted in His own country. (Luke 4:24)

Chapter 5

JESUS was 100 percent Holy God to bring us back to Him.

He is the Savior of Mankind (delivered Mary; Luke 19:10, Isaiah 53)

He turned water to wine in obedience to His mother to honor his own commandment.(John 2:8–10; Exodus 20:12)

He felt virtue went out of Him as His clothing was touched (Mark 5:30; Matthew 14:36; Luke 6:19; Isaiah 11:1–6)

God will wipe away all tears. (Revelation 21:4; Isaiah 25:8)

He promised the Holy Spirit Baptism (John 14:26; Acts 2:1–13; Genesis 1:2)

He said "Come… I will give you rest unto your souls. (Matthew 11:28–30)

He walked on water. He said, "Come." (Matthew 14:25–26; 29)

He said, "whoever drinks of the water that I give shall never thirst." (John 4:14)

He fulfilled Scripture. (Mark 15:28; John 19:28, 36; Isaiah 53)

He is the Lamb whose blood was shed. (Revelation 7:14–17; 12:11; Exodus 12 – Passover)

He did not allow himself to be killed before the appointed time, either passing through their midst or hiding himself. (John 8:59; Luke 4:30; Read Luke 4:28–32.)

The Bible Explained

How Can We Know "The Way"?

I (Jesus) am the way, the truth, and the life: no man comes to the Father, except through Me. If you had known Me, you would have known My Father also: and from now on you know Him, and have seen Him. (John 14:6–7)

God drove man from the Garden of Eden "to guard *the way* to the tree of life" (Genesis 3:24).

In Acts, Christians are called people of *The Way*.

When you know Jesus as Lord, you have *"The Way"*

Chapter 5

What Is "the Truth"?

> It's *not* a booklet nor a pamphlet penned by a group or a man.
> It's *not* a place or an organization anywhere on this land.
> Please, allow Him to repeat, ...

"I am the way, the truth, and the life: No man comes to the Father, except through Me" (John 14:6).

"By this we know the love of God, because *He laid down His life for us*" (I John 3:16).

God the Father is Spirit. God *"laid down His life"* as flesh and blood, Jesus Christ.

The Bible Explained

The Way and the Truth Made Clear

Ask, and it will be given to you; seek, and you will find; knock, and it will be opened to you. (Matthew 7:7)

Be diligent to present yourself approved to God, a worker who does not need to be ashamed, rightly dividing the word of truth. (II Timothy 2:15)

Praying always with all prayer and supplication in the Spirit, being watchful to this end with all perseverance and supplication for all the saints. (Ephesians 6:18)

To obey is better than sacrifice, and to heed than the fat of rams. (I Samuel 15:22)

Chapter 5

What Does He Mean by "The Life"?

> Remember when Adam and Eve disobeyed God? They became spiritually separated from Him by their disobedience and were banished from the Garden of Eden.

"Then the Lord God said, "Behold, the man has become like one of Us, to know good and evil. And now, lest he put out his hand, and take also of the tree of life, and eat, and live forever" therefore the LORD God sent him out of the Garden of Eden… (Genesis 3:22-23)

God did not want them to live forever in the sinful way of life they had chosen. God is a just God, so they had to be punished. However, He is also full of mercy and love. He wanted to give them (and us) another chance to live forever — to choose to be spiritually reunited with Him and reject the god of this world, the devil, who took the form of a serpent in the Garden of Eden.

Jesus Prays for His Disciples

I have revealed You to those whom You gave me out of the world…. they have obeyed Your word…. I pray for them…. protect them by the power of Your name — the name You gave Me — so that they may be one as We are one…. None has been lost except the one doomed to destruction so that Scripture would be fulfilled.... My prayer is not that You take them out of the world but that You protect them from the evil one.... Sanctify them by the Truth; Your Word is Truth. (John 17:6, 9, 11-12, 15, 17 NIV. Read all of John 17)

All of humanity is flawed (under penalty of death) and in need of a *Savior* because of man's sin in the garden. Born-again Christians have chosen *Jesus* as *the Way* back to spiritual union with God and have life in the spirit. The *truth* is that man can live forever because spiritually we have the *life* everlasting.

Genesis to Revelation

Old Testament

Before the fall of man:
"And God said, Let Us make man... after Our likeness..." (Genesis 1:26).

After the fall:
"And the LORD God said... the man is become as one of Us, to know good and evil..." (Genesis 3:22).

During special times... Jesus appeared as the Angel of the LORD (seen in twelve Old Testament Books)

New Testament

Savior, Jesus Christ
Read Matthew, Mark, Luke, and John, the Gospels (Good News).
The Holy Spirit

Chapter 5

"Wait for the promise of the Father... ye shall be baptized with the Holy Ghost" (Acts 2:4).

"And they were all filled with the Holy Ghost..." (Acts 1:4–5).

The Lamb of God
"And looking upon Jesus..., he said, Behold the Lamb of God!" (John 1:36)

". . . Salvation to our God which sitteth upon the throne, and unto the Lamb.... and washed their robes and made them white in the blood of the Lamb" (Revelation 7:10, 14).

"Blessed are they which are called unto the marriage supper of the Lamb" (Revelation 19:9).

***The Old Testament and the
New Testament Fulfilment***

"God said... "I AM WHO *I AM*" (Exodus 3:14).

Jesus said, "Your father Abraham rejoiced to see My day, and he saw it and was glad.... Most assuredly, I say to you, before Abraham was, *I AM*" (John 8:56, 58).
The LORD spoke, "I have heard the complaints of the children of Israel.... in the morning you shall be filled with *bread*. And you shall know that I am the LORD your God." (Exodus 16:11–12)

Jesus said, "I am the living **bread** which came down from heaven: if any man eats of **this bread**, he shall live forever:" (John 6:51)

"The LORD will pass through to strike the Egyptians; and when He sees the blood... the LORD will pass over the door and not allow the destroyer to come into your houses to strike you.... none of you shall go out of *the door* of his house until morning." (Exodus 12:23, 22a)

"Jesus said, 'I am *the door*. If anyone enters by Me, he will be saved, and will go in and out and find pasture'" (John 10:9).

"The LORD is my *shepherd;* I shall not want" (Psalm 23:1).

"Jesus said... 'I am the good shepherd. The good shepherd gives His life for the sheep'" (John 10:7, 11).

And God said, "*Let there be light*"; and there was light. And God saw that the light was good; and God separated the light from the darkness (Genesis 1:3–4).

"The LORD is *my light* and my salvation; Whom shall I fear? The LORD is the strength of my life; Of whom shall I be afraid?" (Psalm 27:1)

"Jesus spoke, 'I am the light of the world. He who follows Me shall not walk in darkness, but have *the light* of life'" (John 8:12).

Chapter 5

Death Pronouncement ". . . till you return to the ground, for out of it you were taken; you are dust, and to *dust you shall return*" (Genesis 3:19).

Everlasting Life Pronouncement Jesus said, "Most assuredly, I say to you, if anyone keeps My word *he shall never see death*" (John 8:51).

Old Testament Guidance: ". . . the LORD went before them by day in a pillar of cloud *to lead the way*, and by night in a pillar of fire to give them light," (Exodus 13:21)

New Testament Guidance: Jesus said, "When He, *the Spirit* of truth, has come, He *will guide you* into all truth;... He will glorify Me" (John 16:13–14).

> "*In the beginning* God created the heavens and the earth" (Genesis 1:1).

> "*In the beginning* was the Word, and the Word was with God, and the Word was God. He was in the beginning with God. All things were made through Him, and without Him nothing was made that was made. In Him was life, and the life was the light of men. And the light shines in the darkness, and the darkness did not comprehend it." (John 1:1–5)

> "And the Word became flesh and dwelt among us, and we beheld His glory, the glory as of the only begotten of the Father, full of grace and truth" (John 1:14).

> "Abraham said, 'My son, God will provide himself *a lamb*'" (Genesis 22:8).

"John saw Jesus coming toward him, and said, 'Behold! *The Lamb* of God who takes away the sin of the world!'" (John 1:29)

Jesus... was baptized and the Holy Spirit descended in bodily form like a dove upon Him, and a voice came from heaven... 'You are My Beloved Son; in You I am well pleased'" (Luke 3:21–22).

"A great multitude which no one could number... crying out with a loud voice, saying, 'Salvation belongs to our God who sits on the throne, and to *the Lamb!*'" (Revelation 7:9–10)

"And the Lord God formed man of the dust of the ground, and *breathed* into his nostrils the breath of life; and man became a living soul" (Genesis 2:7).

"And when He (Jesus) had said this, He *breathed* on them, and said to them, 'Receive the Holy Spirit. If you forgive the sins of any, they are forgiven them: if you retain the sins of any, they are retained.'" (John 20:21–22)

I AM Statements

Jesus is the great *I AM!*
"Jesus said unto him, '*I am* the way, the truth, and the life. No one comes to the Father except through Me'" (John 14:6).
Jesus said, "*I am* with the Father who sent Me.... *I am* One who bears witness of Myself, and the Father who

Chapter 5

sent Me bears witness of Me.... If you had known Me, you would have known My Father also." (John 8:16, 18-19)

Jesus said, "When you lift up the Son of Man, then you will know that *I am He*, and that I do nothing of Myself; but as My Father taught Me, I speak these things" (John 8:28).

And Jesus said, "For judgment *I am* come into this world, that those who do not see may see, and that those who see may be made blind" (John 9:39).

> "Jesus cried out and said, "He who believes in Me, believes not in Me but in Him who sent Me. And *he who sees Me sees Him* who sent Me'" (John 12:44-45).

> "Pilate... said to Him, 'Are You a king then?' Jesus answered, 'You say rightly that *I am* a king. For this cause I was born, and for this cause I have come into the world, that I should bear witness to the truth. Everyone who is of the truth hears My voice.'" (John 18:37)

The Bible Explained

The Bloodline of the Messiah

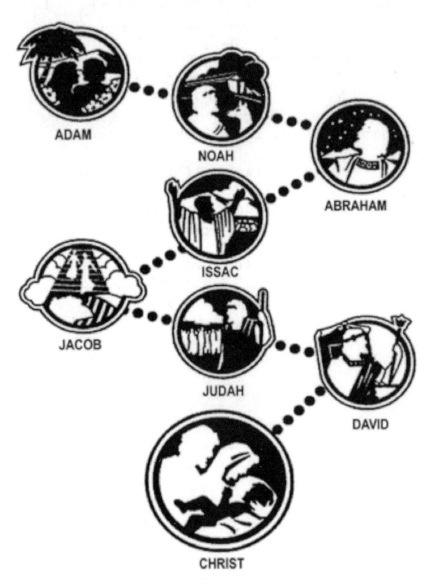

© 1993 by Gospel Light. Permission to photocopy granted.

Chapter 6

SPIRITUAL PROTECTION EXPLAINED

The Invisible Warfare

Clothe yourselves with the Lord Jesus Christ, and do not think about how to gratify the desires of the sinful nature. (Romans 13:14)

The Bible Explained

Understanding Spiritual Warfare and Prayer

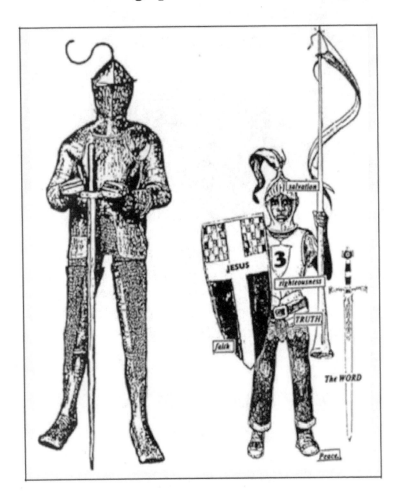

It's a Spiritual Thing

Our battle is not against humanity. Our fight is against unseen forces; the devil, his angels, and the programming of this world.

Chapter 6

"Be strong in the Lord, and in the power of His might" (Ephesians 6:10-12 KJV and NIUV). Continue reading through Ephesians 6:18.

Our fight is against "the prince of the power of the air, the spirit that now works in the sons of disobedience" (Ephesians 2:2).

Spiritual Warfare and Prayer

You are a spiritual being, who has a soul, and lives in a body (tent/earth suit). This section is designed to enable you to gain an understanding of spiritual warfare and how to effectively use the sword of the Spirit, which is the Word of God. It will teach you how and why the spirit and soul of the Christian must be outfitted to stand against the tricks of the devil. The parts of the whole armor of God are for your spiritual body. After dressing, prayer is our very necessary communion with God.

Each New Testament letter describes our dress and Christ-like behavior for battle in the invisible war.

> *Romans 13:12, 14*: "Let us put on the armor of light...
>
> ... put on the Lord Jesus Christ, and make no provision for the flesh, to fulfill its lusts."
>
> *I Corinthians 15:53-54*: "For this corruptible must put on incorruption, and this mortal must put on mortality... Death is swallowed up in victory."
>
> *II Corinthians 10:3-4*: "For though we walk in the flesh, we do not war after the flesh.

For the weapons of our warfare are not carnal but mighty in God for pulling down strongholds."

Galatians 5:27: "For as many of you as have been baptized into Christ have put on Christ."

Ephesians 4:24: "Put on the new man…"

Ephesians 6:11: "Put on the whole armor of God that you may be able to stand your ground in the evil day."

Philippians 3:3: "Rejoice in Christ Jesus, and have no confidence in the flesh,"

Philippians 4:13 NKJV: "I can do all things through Christ who strengthens me."

Colossians 3:10,12–16 NKJV: "Put on the new man… as the elect of God,… put on tender mercies, kindness, humility, meekness, longsuffering; bearing with one another, and forgiving one another… But above all these things put on love, which is the bond of perfection. And let the peace of God rule in your hearts…… . . Let the Word of Christ dwell in you richly."

I Thessalonians 5:8 NKJV: "Be sober, putting on the breastplate of faith and love, and as a helmet the hope of salvation." (Once dressed, verses 9–28 will describe our conduct.)

II Thessalonians 2:13-17 says "Stand fast."

I Timothy 1:18-20 says "Fight the good fight."

II Timothy 2:1-13 says "Be strong in grace."

Titus 2 tells us the *qualities of a sound church* and how to be trained by saving grace. The admonition to *"be sober"* is emphasized.

Philemon18: "Put that on my account."

Hebrews 11 records the Faithful Hall of Fame.

James 4:7 NKJV: "Submit to God. Resist the devil and he will flee from you."

I Peter 5:5, 8 NKJV: "Be clothed with humility: for God resists the proud, and gives grace to the humble.... Be sober, be vigilant; because your adversary the devil walks about like a roaring lion, seeking whom he may devour."

I John 1:7: "Walk in the light…"

I John 2:15-17: Do Not Love the World.

Jude 20: "... praying in the Holy Spirit,"

Revelation 7:14: "... robes… made… white in the blood of the Lamb."

The Bible Explained

How to be Strong and Powerful in the Lord

Dress in the Whole Armor of God
(Ephesians 6:10–18)

T   The top of the **"T" for Truth** is a belt, with the parallel line hanging between his legs. ". . . having girded your loins with truth" (waist).

R   The **"R" for Righteousness** becomes one side of the chest covering. ". . . having put on the breastplate of righteousness."

P   The **"P" for Peace** becomes shoes for the warrior of God. "and having shod your feet with the preparation of the gospel of peace."

F   The **"F" for Faith** is the left side of the shield. "Above all, taking the shield of faith..."

S   The **"S" for Salvation**, is the streamer from the top of the helmet "And take the helmet of salvation..."

W   The **"W" for the Word of God,** is the sword for – ". . . the sword of the Spirit which is the Word of God." It is the only offensive weapon.

THE TRUE VINE

"I am the vine, you are the branches. He who abides in Me, and I in him, bears much fruit; for without Me you can do nothing" (John 15:5).

Chapter 6

Memorize this dress code. You cannot utilize what you do not memorize.

> "Thy Word have I hid in my heart that I might not sin against Thee" (Psalm 119:11).

Natural protection for the body consists of things that can be seen. We are told to walk by FAITH, not by sight. SUPER-natural protection for the spirit and soul consists of things that cannot be seen.

God's Armor is invisible clothing for the body and soul. "For though we walk in the flesh, we do not war according to the flesh: for the weapons of our warfare are not carnal but mighty through God for the pulling down strongholds." II Corinthians 10:3-4

The Whole Armor of God is Jesus Christ

The Helmet of Salvation guard's the mind, the devil's workshop. Jesus is our **SALVATION.** I Thessalonians 5:9

The Breastplate of Righteousness guards the heart; Not the one that beats, but the invisible heart that God, the Holy Spirit speaks through. This is the **righteousness of God through Jesus Christ**, not SELF righteousness. Romans 3:22

The Belt of Truth guards thought processes and dispels the lies perpetrated by the devil, especially those in the category of sexual immorality. Jesus is the way, the **TRUTH,** and the life. John 14:6

Jesus, the Prince of Peace will help feet walk away from discord and mischief, and exhibit love for others. Isaiah 9:5-6

FAITH in Jesus Christ. Without faith, you cannot please God. He's our protection from and during satanic attacks. Hebrews 11

Jesus is the WORD of God. Jesus used "it is written" to thwart the devil during His encounter. We must use it also. Matthew 4:1-11 "In the beginning was the Word, and Word was with God, and the Word was God. ... And the Word became flesh..." John1:1,14

Chapter 6

Jesus is God in flesh.

IT'S A SPIRITUAL THING!

Our battle is not against any person. Our fight is against unseen forces; the devil, his angels, and the programming of this world. As stated in Paul's letter to Ephesus:

> Be strong in the Lord, and in the power of His might… For we are not wrestling with flesh and blood, [contending with physical opponents], but against the despotisms, against the powers, against [the master spirits who are] the world rulers of this present darkness, against spiritual forces of wickedness in the heavenly (supernatural) sphere. (Ephesians 6:10–12 Amplified)

Dress in the whole armor of God, Jesus Christ, and God will fight your battle for you. Read the Bible stories to see how He helped others.

Use Spiritual Discernment

Beware of Antichrist Deceivers (II John 7–9).

Ask, *"Is Jesus Christ LORD?"*
If the answer is not "Yes," you have three options.
1. Teach them the Truth,
2. Pray and walk away, or
3. Walk away and pray!

> "Be still, and know that I am God: I will be exalted among the heathen, I will be exalted in the earth" (Psalm 46:10).

"... to the praise of the glory of His grace, wherein He hath made us accepted in the Beloved" (Ephesians 1:6).

**Everyone fights a
SPIRITUAL BATTLE! It is out of sight!
Every day, *(in your mind,)* dress your spirit in
THE WHOLE ARMOR OF GOD,
JESUS CHRIST.**

MEMORIZE THIS
SPIRITUAL DRESSWEAR!
"We do not wrestle against flesh and blood, but against..." the devil, his angels, and the New World Order! (Read all of Ephesians 6:10-18)

God has defeated Satan and will deliver us from the guerrilla warfare if we dress for the battle. We have been transferred from darkness to light, but it is our responsibility to "put on" our spiritual armor, Jesus.

Chapter 6

How to Memorize the Word Faster, More Thoroughly, and More Effectively

The Word says "may your whole spirit, and soul, and body be kept blameless at the coming of our Lord Jesus Christ" (I Thessalonians 5:23). The body (physical), soul (emotions), and spirit (the mind and heart) are involved in the process of memorization of the Word. When our spirit man is clothed in Jesus, the whole armor of God, our helper, the Holy Spirit will assure remembrance of the Word.

To facilitate memorization, underline the one word in The Lies list, and the opposite word(s) in The Truth column. Remember the *truth* word, and then add Jesus, Christ, or God. The other words will fall into place, based on context. Input and utilize the sword of the Spirit, the Word of God.

The sufferings of life's exertion are not worthy to be compared with the glory that will be revealed to those who exercise the Word. Count it all joy. Run in such a way that you may win the prize, which is the crown of everlasting life.

To learn much more about
Spiritual Warfare and Prayer, download the
Chip Ingram App
Listen to his series on
The Invisible War:
"Living on The Edge"
Enjoy many other important teachings.

The Bible Explained

The Sword of the Spirit — The Word of God
My Never-Again List

The Lies	The Truth	Scripture
Never again will I confess "I can't."	For I can do all things through Christ who strengthens me.	Phil. 4:13
Never again will I confess lack,	For My God shall supply all of my needs according to His riches in glory by Christ Jesus.	Phil 4:19
Never again will I confess fear.	For God hath not given me the spirit of fear, but of power, and of love, and of a sound mind (self-control).	Tim. 1:7
Never again will I confess doubt (lack of faith).	For God hath given to every man the measure of faith.	Rom 12:3
Never again will I confess weakness.	For The Lord is the strength of my life. For the people that know their God shall be strong and do exploits.	Psalm 27:1 Dan. 11:32
Never again will I confess supremacy of Satan over my life.	For greater is He that is in me that he that is in the world.	John 4:4
Never again will I confess defeat,	For God always causeth me to triumph in Christ Jesus.	Cor. 2:14
Never again will I confess lack of wisdom,	for Christ Jesus is made unto me wisdom from God.	I Cor. 1:30

Chapter 6

Never again will I confess worries and frustrations,	for I am Casting all my cares upon Him who careth for me. (In Christ I am care-free.)	I Pet. 5:7
Never again will I confess bondage,	for Where the Spirit of the Lord is, there is liberty. My body is the temple of the Holy Spirit.	II Cor. 3:17 I Cor. 6:19
Never again will I confess condemnation,	for There is therefore now no condemnation to them which are in Christ Jesus. I am in Christ; therefore, I am free from condemnation.	Rom. 8:1
Never again will I confess loneliness,	Jesus said, Lo, I am with you always, even unto the end of the world. And I will never leave thee, nor forsake thee.	Matt. 28:20 Heb. 13:5
Never again will I confess curses or bad luck,	for Christ hath redeemed us from the curse of the law, being made a curse for us: that the blessing of Abraham might come on the gentiles through Jesus Christ; that we might receive the promise of the Spirit through faith.	Gal. 3:13–14
Never again will I confess discontent,	because I have learned, in whatsoever state (circumstances) I am, therewith to be content.	Phil. 4:11
Never again will I confess confusion,	because God is not the author of confusion, but of peace. And We have received, not the spirit of the world, but the spirit is of God: that we might know the things that are freely given to us of God.	I Cor. 14:33

Never again will I confess persecution,	for, If God be for us, who can be against us?	Rom 8:31
Never again will I confess the dominion of sin over my life,	because The Law of the Spirit of life in Christ Jesus hath made me free from the law of sin and death. and As far as the east is from the west, so far hath He removed our transgressions from us.	Rom. 8:2 Ps. 103:12
Never again will I confess insecurity,	because When though liest down, thou Shalt not be afraid: Yea, thou shalt lie down, and thy sleep shall be sweet… for the Lord shall be thy confidence, and shall keep thy foot from being taken.	Prov. 3:24–26
Never again will I confess failure,	because Nay, in all things we are more than conquerors through Him that loved us.	Rom. 8:37

Test yourself! Look up the *Truth* for the words frustration, fear of the future, troubles, etc.

The Pathways to Love, Peace, and Joy

Trust in the Lord with all your heart and lean not to your own understanding; In all your ways acknowledge Him, and He will make your paths straight. Do not be wise in your own eyes; fear the Lord and shun evil. This will bring health to your body and nourishment to your bones. (Proverbs 3:5–8)

Chapter 6

1. Memorize the Swords of the Spirit and the scripture above.
2. When the devil gives you a thought, say aloud, "That's not my thought!"

Then immediately replace it with the appropriate sword of the Spirit, which is the Word of God that now abides (has taken up residency) in your spirit (See John 15:4–10). Repeat it several times if necessary. Repetition works! That is the reason songs have familiar beats, repetitious words, and choruses. Sing your favorite Christian song. Use the Word to fight your spiritual battles. The devil hates praise, prayer, and the Word. Make him flee from you (James 4:7).

Easy? No! But It Is Worth It!

It Takes Work, but much less work than losing sleep, worrying, and fretting all the time (I Peter 5:7).

It Takes Work because it is contrary to what we have been programmed by the world to think and say. Addictions don't die easily. "Not as the world gives do I give to you" (John 14:27).

It Takes Work, but we must overthrow those old strongholds (thought patterns), and replace them with the

Word of God. We can do all things through Christ who strengthens us (Philippians 4:13).

It Takes Work, but blessings will follow. He will keep in perfect peace whose mind is stayed on Him (Isaiah 26:3). There are rewards that await the blessed (Matthew 5:3–12).

It Takes Work, but it is written: "work out your own salvation with fear and trembling" (Philippians 2:12).

You can't break God's promises by standing on them. They will lift you up. You shall mount up with wings as eagles; run and not be weary; walk and not faint (Isaiah 40:31).

Example:

The devil says things like: "How are you going to pay those bills? That gang will attack you. You shouldn't have helped that person. You should not _____. You cannot be free from drugs. Get even with _____. He (she/they) can't do that to you! You won't be forgiven this time. Write your own statement of lies that the devil is telling you. _____
Tell the devil aloud, "That is not my thought!" Now replace that thought with the Word of God, aloud.

In answer to the lies of the devil, God's Word says: God shall supply all your needs according to His riches in glory by Christ Jesus. He shall deliver you from the snare of the fowler. Give, and it shall be given unto you. Vengeance is mine, I will repay. Count it all joy… Rejoice… through trials… Glory in tribulations… Ask. Your sins are forgiven. Fill in the blank with God's word for your needs.

When the devil troubles your mind, God's word says, think on specific things. Decide on your own set of Godly things to "think on," and fill in the blanks. Remember them by memorizing the bold type to recite aloud when you are under spiritual attack. (My sets are in brackets as examples.)

Whatsoever Things Are True [Jesus loves me, this I know!]

Chapter 6

Whatsoever Things Are Honorable; [Write a note or send a card to a sick or depressed person friend. Write a thank you note. Call to lift someone's spirits. Tell them Jesus loves them. Do a good deed, etc.]

Whatsoever Things Are Just; [Read Psalm 11 or 73; Confidence in God's concern for justice.]

Whatsoever Things Are Pure; [I think of a baby's or a best friend's smile.]

Whatsoever Things Are Lovely; [The love of my family, my sister, my sisters and brothers in Christ at Cascade UMC Disciple I Bible study and my senior citizen mothers and fathers at QLS Bible study. Listening to and singing with my favorite praise songs, etc.]

Whatsoever Things Are Of Good Report; [You are reading these pathways, and any other good news that you can think of, etc.]

If There Is Any Virtue; [Our bodies are temples of the Holy Spirit. The enthusiastic bright-eyed presence of my seniors and their love for the Lord.]

If There Is Any Praise; [Look in the list of psalms of praise and read a chapter of praise aloud!]

Think on these things! The God of peace will be with you.

Memorize this list. It is part of the arsenal to help you fight the spiritual battles that are certain to come.

> Finally, brethren, whatsoever things are true, whatsoever things are honest, whatsoever things are just, whatsoever things are

> pure, whatsoever things are lovely, whatsoever things are of good report; if there be any virtue, and ithere be any praise, think on these things. (Philippians 4:8)

These seven qualities create an environment of peace:

True is giving ethical "truthfulness."
Noble/Honest/Honorable is to be respected.
Just is giving people what they deserve.
Pure is holy in relation to God.
Lovely is attractive.
Of Good Report is praiseworthy.
Virtue refers to moral excellence
Praiseworthy is something that brings God praise.
The God of Peace complements "the peace of God" in that life with these characteristics encourages God's presence.
Think on these things!
The God of peace will be with you.

> Be anxious for nothing, but with prayer and supplication, with thanksgiving let our requests be made known to God; and the peace of God... will guard our hearts and minds through Christ Jesus. (Philippians 4:6-7)

If you're going to worry, don't pray.
If you're going to pray, don't worry.

Write your responses in the blank spaces.
We shall believe the report of the Lord!

Whatsoever things are **true**:

___

Chapter 6

Whatsoever things are **honest/honorable**:

Whatsoever things are **just**:

Whatsoever things are **pure**:

Whatsoever things are **lovely**:

Whatsoever things are of **good report**:

If there is any **virtue**:

If there is any **praise**:

Think on these things!

Memorize your responses *before* a demonic attack and then pray. Ask God to grant your requests. Give God praise and thanksgiving. The peace of God will keep your heart and mind through Christ Jesus.

The Bible Explained

To Have Peace And Joy, You Must Love And Forgive

A new commandment I give to you, that you love one another; as I have loved you, that you also love one another. By this all will know that you are My disciples, if you have love for one another. (John 15:34-35 NKJV)

Judge not, and you shall not be judged. Condemn not, and you shall not be condemned. Forgive, and you will be forgiven. (Luke 6:37 NKJV)

Chapter 6

Peace I leave with you, My peace I give to you; not as the world gives do I give to you. Let not your heart be troubled, neither let it be afraid. (John 14:27 NKJV)

Do not sorrow, for the joy of the Lord is your strength. (Nehemiah 8:10 NKJV)

My Testimony

God *formed* man from the dust of the earth. (Genesis 2:7)

Man sinned. (Genesis 3:6-7). God loved and knew me before He *formed* me in my mother's womb (Psalm 139:12-16).

Although fearfully and wonderfully made, without being spiritually *informed* of the Way to the Truth (John 8:32), sin *deformed* me, and I *conformed* to the world's ways (Romans 12:2).

After being "knocked off my high horse" (… *ouch*,… *Halleluiah*,) by the Light (Acts 9:3-4), I gave up my right to control myself and submitted to my Husband. The Lord of hosts is His name (Isaiah 54:5).

I prayed and received salvation (Romans 10:9) and peace (Philippians 4:7).

The Word of Truth *transformed* my mind and I am *reformed* by Grace, avoiding increased punishment (Leviticus 26:23-24).

I use my spiritual gifts (1 Corinthians 12) with love (1 Corinthians 13:4–8), dressed in my *uniform*, the Whole Armor of God, and worship Him through Jesus Christ for His *reformation*.

I am a "Warrior for the Lord"!

(My theme song, sung by Marilyn McCoo) Praise be to God; I am Blessed!

Chapter 7

CHRIST ESTEEM
(Not *SELF* ESTEEM)
EXPLAINED

Self?

But mark this: There will be terrible times in the last days. People will be lovers of themselves (II Timothy 3:1–2) (Read all of II Timothy 3)

The Bible Explained

Everybody Needs Love

God demonstrates His own love toward us, in that while we were still sinners, Christ died for us. (Romans 5:8)

"Jesus loves me, this I know!" This song has such very special significance to me because I sang it to my sister as she lay in her hospital bed dying from leukemia. I personalized it to her by changing the word "me" to "you."

I learned all the words to the song in my childhood and did not realize what they meant until the moment I sang them to Lillian. Not since childhood had I sang it to completion. As I sang, I was torn between the joy (in the spirit) of knowing where she was going, and the torment of torrential tears (the flesh) because I was losing her as my earthly companion. All the words to "Jesus Loves Me" came back to my memory as I sang. "But the Comforter, which is the Holy Spirit... shall bring all things to your remembrance" (John 14:26).

Dennis DeHaan wrote in *Our Daily Bread*, "From the cradle to the grave, we all need love."

How vividly this is illustrated in the song "Jesus Loves Me" by Anna B. Warner (1824–1915). She and her sister Susan were gifted novelists. Anna also published many poems. The familiar lines of "Jesus Loves Me" were penned in 1860 as a poem of comfort spoken to a dying child in one of Susan's stories. Today it's sung by children and adults around the world.

Jesus' love is so important because His love is not some sentimental, easygoing acceptance of sinners. It's a sacrificial love that absolved us from our guilt and took the burden of our sins when He died on the cross for us.

Jesus' love is so important because He is God in the flesh. And only He can meet our deepest longing — our lifelong need for love (Romans 5:8–21).

Chapter 7

"Holy, Holy, Holy" is another song I sang to Lillian as she was leaving to go and be with the Lord. Lillian, Janet, and I had planned to sing it to Daddy for Father's Day the next month, and I told her how much we would miss her beautiful voice. Knowing Jesus Christ as God the Son and that He loved us was all that mattered at that moment. "Holy, Holy, Holy" was played as the processional for her funeral, and Daddy's three years to the week later.

Knowing how much Jesus loves us is also important because we are all dying children. There is no greater solace on this earth than knowing there is a home in heaven that awaits those of us who accept Jesus Christ as Lord.

The greatest single thought that ever crossed my mind is "Jesus loves me, this I know, for the Bible tells me so."

> "Except you become as little children, you
> shall not enter into the kingdom of heaven"
> (Matthew 18:3).

The Bible Explained

"Casting all your cares on Him;... He cares for you" (I Peter 5:7).

Chapter 7

You Are Special

God said You are special in His Word.

"The spirit of man is the candle of the Lord, searching all the inmost parts of his being" (Proverbs 20:27).

God Loves You So Much!

"For God so loved the world that He gave His only begotten Son, that whosoever believeth in Him Should not perish, but have everlasting life" (John 3:16).

The Bible Explained

Do Great Things for Jesus' Sake!

Let nothing hinder you! Say every day, "I can do all things through Christ who strengthens me" (Philippians 4:13).

Just make sure,
"what ever you do,
do all to the glory of God"
(I Corinthians 10:31).

Chapter 7
So what if you make a mistake?

First, forgive others.
Second, humble yourself.
Third, ask God to forgive you.
If you mean it with all your heart
and say you won't do it again,
God will forgive you!

Forgive us our debts, as we forgive our debtors. (Matthew 6:12)

God resists the proud, but gives grace to the humble. (James 4:6)

I acknowledged my sin unto You, and my iniquity I have not hid… and You forgave the iniquity of my sin. (Psalm 32:5)

Blessed child of the King, praise God!
Because you know Jesus is Lord,
you are perfect in Christ Jesus.

You are the apple of Jesus' eye!

"Keep My commandments, and live; and My law as the apple of your eye" (Proverbs 7:2).

Since you know Jesus is God in the flesh, you are not fooled!

"The fool has said in his heart, "there is no God" (Psalm 14:1).

As we learn and grow in faith, we will be more Christlike as we conform to His image. The Helper will teach us (John 14:26). All of God's children are destined for greatness! You are an amazingly remarkable formation of God! Daily say: "I am fearfully and wonderfully made: a marvelous work of God" (Psalm 139:14).

After you choose Jesus as Lord of your life, your friends might say you act weird, or at least sort of different. Smile, and then tell them the correct terminology is *"peculiar."*

You are... a peculiar people. (I Peter 2:9)

Chapter 7

Do not be conformed to this world: but be transformed by the renewing of your mind, that you may prove what is that good, and acceptable, and perfect, will of God. (Romans 12:2)

Christian Formation, Spiritual Formation, Faith Formation and Family Formation. Intergenerational Development for Congregational Christian Perfection is described:

> From whom the whole body, joined and held together by every joint with which it is equipped, when each part is working properly, makes the body grow so that it builds itself up in love. (Ephesians 4:16)

Respect the Christ in You!

Rethink Church! It's not only the house of worship, but *we* are the church and must open our hearts, minds, and doors to others and the Truth. God formed man from the dust in the likeness of Jesus, breathed His Spirit into him, and man became a living soul (See Genesis 2:7). God is Spirit; thus when God breathed into him, Adam and all later human beings became a unique mix of the physical and spiritual. Therefore, "let us consider one another in order to stir up love and good works, not forsaking the assembling of ourselves together." (Hebrews 10:24–25)

The Bible Explained

"Do you not know that your body is a temple of the
Holy Spirit, who is in you,
whom you have received from God?
You are not your own; you were bought at a price.
Therefore honor God with your body."
(I Corinthians 6:19–20)

Chapter 7

Free at Last

True freedom can only be obtained through Jesus Christ. We must allow the fruit of the spirit: love, joy, peace, longsuffering, gentleness, goodness, faith, meekness, and temperance to work in us. If the Son makes you free, you will be free indeed. Like a kite, a Christian can rise the highest when the winds of adversity blow the hardest. Welcome adversity as a means of growth. Want nothing more than to know God and His will, fulfilling His good purposes. Hold to God in faith. One day you will see that He was upon the wings of the wind. You can be happy because the Word says "Happy is he who has the God of Jacob for his help, whose hope is in the Lord his God." Trusting and obeying the Lord brings true happiness. Trust in man or oneself will bring pain and disappointment. Love and trust God. Love and forgive man. Rejoice, even through tears; be glad and filled with the joy of the Lord. When we rejoice through many trials, while being tried by fire, we shall come forth as gold. Salvation is through Jesus Christ. We cannot save ourselves.

Beliefs other than Christianity are works-based. They must *do* this, *do* that or *do* the other to be acceptable to their god or membership. Our belief is faith based and simply requires that the believer must be born again (in the spirit) to see the kingdom of God. We must confess with our mouths and believe in our hearts that Jesus is God. That's all! Do... do... do... versus done! Jesus said, *"It is finished."* What freedom!

How to Recognize and Avoid New Age Deception

New Age philosophy teaches one to empower and exalt oneself. God wants our lives sacrificed to Him. Our physical death is of no benefit to Him. He wants us dead to self, and that death to self becomes a living sacrifice. Our role is not to strive for self-assertiveness, self-consciousness, self-consideration, self-indulgence, self-interest, self-pity, self-realization, self-sufficiency, self-vindication, self-understanding, self-esteem, or anything that pertains to self.

> For I say, through the grace given unto me, to every man that is among you, not to think of himself more highly than he ought to think; but to think soberly, according as God has dealt to every man the measure of faith. (Romans 12:3)

> Come unto me, all ye that labour and are heavy laden, and I will give you rest. Take my yoke upon you, and learn of me; for I am meek and lowly in heart: and ye shall find rest unto your souls. For my yoke is easy and my burden is light. (Matthew 11:28–30).

Jesus said come, *take my yoke*, and *learn of me*. The only way to learn of Him is to study the Word. The spiritual understanding is not intellect, but comes by prayer, denying self, obedient discipline, and being humble.

> If my people who are called by my name, shall humble themselves, and pray, and seek my face, and turn from their wicked ways; then will I hear from heaven, and will forgive their sin, and will heal their land. (II Chronicles 7:14)

Chapter 7

Use the Sword of the Spirit, which is the Word of God to fight your battles. It is the only offensive weapon on the whole armor of God. The remainder is defensive.

Since "self" thoughts feed the flesh, they cannot be of God, who is Spirit. The Word feeds the Spirit.

> Walk in the Spirit, and ye shall not fulfill the lust of the flesh. For the flesh lusteth against the Spirit and the Spirit against the flesh. And these are contrary the one to the other; so that ye cannot do the things ye would. (Galatians 5:16-17).

About "self," Jesus said: "If any man will come after me, let him deny himself; take up his cross, and follow me" (Matthew 16:24).

In regard to esteem, He said, "Let nothing be done through strife or vain glory; but in lowliness of mind. Let each esteem other better than themselves" (Philippians 2:3).

"Esteem them very highly in love for their works sake. And be at peace among yourselves" (I Thessalonians 5:13).

The battle must be fought, based on giving up our rights to natural independence, our self-assertiveness, and ourselves. The natural life is not spiritual. It can only be made spiritual by the sacrifice of one's self. Romans 12:1 states it this way: "I beseech you therefore, brethren... present your bodies a living sacrifice, holy, acceptable unto God, which is your reasonable service."

Our Lord's teaching is always anti-self. He wants us to be exactly like Himself, and the characteristic of the Son of God is self-expenditure.

To be His disciple, self-interest, pride, and self-sufficiency must be completely erased. He wants us to be sanctified—Himself in me. Then, what about "yourself"?

Jesus said:

The Bible Explained

Lay not up for yourselves treasures upon earth. (Matthew 6:19)

Dearly Beloved, avenge not yourselves. (Romans 12:19)

Give yourselves to fasting and prayer. (I Corinthians 7:5)

Examine yourselves as to whether you are in the faith. Test yourselves. Do ou not know yourselves, that Jesus Christ is in you? —-unless indeed you are disqualified. (II Corinthians 13:5)

Speaking to yourselves in psalms and hymns and Spiritual songs."

(Ephesians 5:19)

Wherefore comfort yourselves together, edify one another… and be at peace among yourselves. (I Thessalonians 5:11-13)

Humble yourselves therefore under the mighty hand of God, that he may exalt you in due time. (I Peter 5:6)

Building up yourselves on your most holy faith, praying in the Holy Ghost, keep yourselves in the Love of God looking for the mercy of our Lord Jesus Christ unto eternal life. (Jude 1: 20-21)

In the fear of the Lord, I obediently did as I was instructed. I put aside everything and did "seek… first

Chapter 7

the Kingdom of God." The fruit of the Spirit: love, joy, and peace are now mine. I thought I was prepared many times to receive all the things He said shall be added, "But when it pleased God..."

"But When It Pleased God..."

(Inspired by "Leave Room for God" from the January 25 reading in *My Utmost for His Highest* by Oswald Chambers). Galatians 1:11-17, paraphrased and personalized.

For I would have you know, Brothers and Sisters, that the Spiritual Pathways, which were written by me are not man's pathways. For I did not receive them from man, nor was I taught them, but they came to me through a revelation from Jesus Christ (via the Holy Spirit). For you have heard of my former life in my hometown and hear how I passed around teachings other than Christ's, took yoga to learn to relax and spoke foul-mouthed about anything that went contrary to the way I felt it should be — while professing to be a Christian and therefore nullifying my profession. I was full of *self*. I gave away many New Age books and got the attention of many, so zealous was I for the quest for peace of mind. But when He who set me apart before I was born and had called me through His grace,... But when it pleased God to reveal the *Pathways to Love, Peace and Joy* to me through His Spirit in order that I could write this Journal, I did not confer with flesh and blood, nor did I ask any minister's opinion, but instead, wrote it down — recorded it with joy unspeakable. Thank you Jesus!

> "To everything there is a season, and a time to every purpose under the heaven" (Ecclesiastes 3:1).

Chapter 8

SUPERNATURAL GRACE

Grace Personified

"For God so loved the world, that He gave His only begotten son, that whosoever believes in Him should not perish but have everlasting life" (John 3:16)

The Bible Explained

Amazing Grace

Our God of Grace is Jesus Christ.

Chapter 8

> "In Him we have redemption through His blood, the forgiveness of sins, according to the riches of His grace" (Ephesians 1:7).

It's hard to shake off a mother's influence. John Newton's earliest memories were of his godly mother who, despite fragile health, devoted herself to nurturing his soul. Though she died when he was seven, he later recalled her tearful prayers for him.

After her death, Newton alternated between boarding school and the high seas, desiring to live a good life but nonetheless falling deeper and deeper into sin. More voyages, dangers, and snares followed. Then on the night of March 9, 1748, Newton, at age twenty-three, was jolted awake by a brutal storm that descended too suddenly for the crew to foresee. The next day, he cried to the Lord. The next several years saw slow, halting spiritual growth in Newton and in the end he became one of British's most powerful evangelical preachers and author of hundreds of hymns.

Here's something you may not know about Newton's most famous hymn. The title wasn't originally "Amazing Grace" but "Faith's Review and Expectation." It is based in Newton's study of I Chronicles 17:16–17.

(Excerpts from "Then Sings My Soul" by Robert J. Morgan)

Grace: we have, God's Righteousness At Christs' Expense.

The great miracle of the grace of God is that He forgives sin, and it is the death of Jesus Christ alone that enables the divine nature to forgive and remain true to itself in doing so. The grace of God is absolute and limitless, and the work of salvation through Jesus is complete and finished forever.

The Bible Explained

For Interpersonal Relationships

Some of the things that happen to us have nothing to do with us. God is getting us into fellowship with Himself to use us for His purposes. God brings us into circumstances to educate our faith. God opens ways for fellowship with His Son so that we might get close to and learn of Him and how He works in and with us, then comfort with the comfort with which we have been comforted. Pray, accept, and be obedient to the Word. By obedience we understand the nature of God. Show empathy and do not seek revenge.

Seek Christian spiritual counseling to overcome the difficulties, and learn to love others as God loves us. Beware of pride—self-reliance that works toward an imagined lack of need for God.

Do not judge one another, but forgive and love. There will be change, even though we will experience the biggest change in ourselves because the Word will be causing a transformation. New wine is best preserved when placed in new skins. The newfound ability to persevere in circumstances that were totally unacceptable is evidence that the Word of God works.

Listen to Godly counsel and accept instruction that you may gain wisdom and understanding for the future. However, be cautious about interfering in the lives of others, family members included. Our part is to be so rightly related and in tune to God that His discernment flows through us all the time for the blessing of another person. An example is that "Peter asked... 'Lord, what about him?' Jesus answered, 'If I want him to remain alive until I return, what is that to you? You follow me'" (John 21:21–22).

Chapter 8

Relationships

"Behold, to obey is better than sacrifice, and to heed than the fat of rams. For rebellion is as witchcraft, and stubbornness is as iniquity and idolatry" (I Samuel 15:22-23).

The Bible has specific instructions on how we are to relate to one another. The Ten Commandments are in the Old Testament at Exodus 20:3-17 and Deuteronomy 5:6-21. In the New Testament, Jesus said, "A new commandment I give to you, that you love one another; as I have loved you... By this all will know that you are My disciples, if you have love for one another" (John 13:34-35). Love is the fulfilment of the law.

Jesus reduced the Law, the Ten Commandments of the Old Testament, to love—one commandment in the New Testament. If the love of God is shed abroad in your heart, you will be able to fulfill the law.
1. Love to God will admit no other god.
2. Love will not debase the object it adores.
3. Love to God will never dishonor His Name.
4. Love to God will reverence His day.
5. Love to parents will honor them.
6. Hate, not love, is a murderer.
7. Lust, not love, commits adultery.
8. Love will give, but never steals.
9. Love will not slander nor lie.
10. Love's eye is not covetous.

For Study:

Principles Underlying the *Ten* Commandments
   1. **Faith and Loyalty** — Hebrews 11:6; Matthew 4:8-10
   2. **Worship** — Jeremiah 10:10-12; Psalm 115:3-8; Revelation 14:6, 7

3. **Reverence** — Psalm 111:9; 89:7; Hebrews 12:28; II Timothy 2:19
4. **Holiness or Sanctification and Consecration** — I Peter 1:15, 16; Hebrews 12:14; Exodus 31:13; Ezekiel 20:12; I Corinthians 1:30; Proverbs 3:6
5. **Obedience, or Respect for Authority** — Ephesians 6:1–3; Colossians 3:20; II Kings 2:23, 24
6. **Love** — Leviticus 19:17; I John 3:15; Matthew 5:21–26, 43–48
7. **Purity** — Matthew 5:8; Ephesians 5:3, 4; Colossians 3:5, 6; I Timothy 5:22; I Peter 2:11
8. **Honesty** — Romans 12:17; Ephesians 4:28; II Thessalonians 3:10–12
9. **Truthfulness** — Ephesians 4:25; Colossians 3:9; Proverbs 6:16–19; 12:19; Revelation 21:27; 22:15
10. **Contentment and Unselfishness** — Ephesians 5:5; Colossians 3:5; I Timothy 6:6–11; Hebrews 13:5

The agape love that God wants us to have in relation to one another is found in I Corinthians 13. This chapter, called the Hymn of Love, beautifully explains the way to use our spiritual gifts. Gifts without love are poor things. People talk about love, but they do not live it.

Until the love of Christ is in a heart, it is impossible for men to love one another with any degree of permanency. Men seem to worship force. But history shows us that the victories of force do not last. "There is a way that seems right to a man, but its end is the way of death" (Proverbs 16:25).

Read the Love Chapter
I Corinthians 13

Read aloud slowly, inserting your name in the blank spaces. The Holy Spirit will affirm or deny the Truth and

Chapter 8

show areas in your life that need prayer and application of the Word.

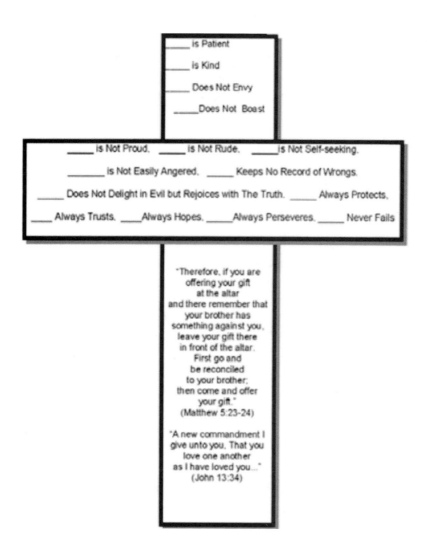

Jesus Christ is love. God wants us to be all agape love is. For more relationship help, study I Corinthians 7 and Colossians 3.

"For God so loved the world that He gave his only begotten Son, that whosoever believes in Him should not perish, but have everlasting life" (John 3:16).

There is a *3:16 LOVE Syndrome* present in almost every New Testament Book! Read I John 3:16, then check them all out!

Christian Conduct

From the **Bible**
The **B**asic **I**nstruction **B**efore **L**eaving **E**arth
Family Responsibilities

For Children:

Children, obey your parents in the Lord: for this is right. "Honor your father and mother," which is the first commandment with promise: "That it may be well with you and you may live long on earth" (Ephesians 6:1–3; Deuteronomy 5:16). Each of you shall give due respect to his mother and his father, and keep My Sabbaths holy. I the Lord am your God. (Leviticus 19:3 Amplified)

For Fathers:

And you, fathers, do not provoke your children to wrath, but bring them up in the training and admonition of the Lord. Fathers, do not provoke your children, lest they become discouraged. (Ephesians 6:4, Colossians 3:21)

Chapter 8

For Wives:
> Wives, be submissive to your own husbands, that even if some do not obey the word, they, without a word, may be won by the conduct of their wives, when they observe your chaste conduct accompanied by fear... the hidden person of the heart, with the incorruptible beauty of a gentle and quiet spirit, which is very precious in the sight of God. As Sarah... whose daughters you are if you do good and are not afraid with any terror. (I Peter 3:1-2, 4-6; Read Proverbs 31:10-31 for the description of the virtuous woman, a worthy woman, the wife of noble character.)

For Husbands:
> Husbands, love your wives and do not be bitter toward them... dwell with them with understanding, giving honor to the wife, as to the weaker vessel... that your prayers may not be hindered... love your wives, just as Christ also loved the church, and gave Himself for her... so husbands ought to love their own wives as their own bodies; he who loves his wife loves himself. For no one ever hated his own flesh, but nourishes and cherishes it, just as the Lord does the church. (Colossians 3:19, I Peter 3:7, Ephesians 5:25, 28-29)

For Older Women:
> The older women likewise, that they be reverent in behavior, not slanderers, not given to much wine, teachers of good things — that they admonish the young women to

love their husbands, to love their children, to be discreet, chaste, homemakers, sober-minded, in all things showing yourself to be a pattern of good works; in doctrine showing integrity, reverence, incorruptibility, sound speech that cannot be condemned that one who is an opponent may be ashamed, having nothing evil to say of you. (Titus 2:3-8)

For Older Men:
Be sober, reverent, temperate, sound in faith, in love, in patience. (Titus 2:2)

Marriage:
Jesus... said... from the beginning of the creation God made them male and female. For this cause shall a man leave his father and his mother, and shall cleave to his wife: and they shall be one flesh. What therefore God has joined together, let not man put asunder. (Mark 10:5-9)

God hates divorce. (See Malachi 2:14-16) In as much as it is within you, be at peace with all. God wants us to work at cleansing ourselves from all filthiness of the flesh and spirit, perfecting holiness in the fear of the Lord. "For your Maker is our husband, the Lord God Almighty is His name. The LORD will call you back as if you were a wife deserted and distressed in spirit, a wife who married young, only to be rejected... I will have compassion on you." (See Isaiah 54:5-7, and Genesis 3 for greater understanding.)

Chapter 8

Genesis 3:16 (KJV) is one of the "hardest sayings" in the Bible; it is woman's punishment from God for eating the forbidden fruit.

> Unto the woman He said, I will greatly multiply thy sorrow and thy conception; in sorrow thou shalt bring forth children; and thy desire shall be to thy husband, and he shall rule over thee.

Her "desire" has less to do with eroticism than it does with a woman's natural desire to lead/rule/boss her husband, having her way above all else. The verb "to rule over" does not express God's order for husbands in their relationships to their wives. *Hard Sayings of the Bible*, by Kaiser, Davids, Bruce, and Brauch states:

> The sense of Genesis 3:16 is simply this: Because of her sin, Eve would turn away from her sole dependence on God and turn now to her husband. The results would not at all be pleasant, warned God, as He announced this curse.

If the spouse finds it too difficult to submit to the earthly partner, submit to the heavenly Husband, the Lord God of Hosts. Do as He says. Be obedient to the Word, because obedience is better than sacrifice. Disobedience to covenant relationships may cost more than you want to pay.

The woman's punishment is directly related to man. Man's punishment (Genesis 3:17–19) is directly related to his work, not woman. However, his punishment was not only for eating the forbidden fruit, but because he listened to his wife instead of obeying God. That is the reason Paul said women are to submit, *respect,* admire, lead her husband without a word by her demeanor. Men are to not be bitter, but *love* and protect their wives, and submit also (read I Peter 3). The New Testament writers are simply trying to make marriage easier by telling the man and the woman to do the hard or unnatural thing. No punishment seems pleasant at the time it is administered, yet later brings peace and righteousness to those who obey the Word of God (see Hebrews 12:11–12).

In the Great Commission, Jesus said we are to make disciples of all men. If discipleship is to be believed abroad, it must begin at home. The world and our children are watching. God hates pride. He resists the proud and exalts the humble. Focus on the Word and not on the circumstances. Jesus washed the feet of Judas. He died for our sins while we were yet sinners. He wants us to *love and forgive,* and lead others to Him by our actions and, if necessary, use words. Living faithful lives is our best witness. We may be the only "Bible" some people will read.

There may be irreconcilable differences. However, have you considered that the same two "different" people once loved one another enough to marry? What may appear to be horrible incompatibility may just be two people who are fantastically complementary. Remember what attracted you to your spouse. Perhaps you can love and respect that attribute. Learn to yield to your partner's likes, dislikes, and wishes, and yield to the Spirit. JOY comes from placing **J**esus first, **O**thers next, and **Y**ourself last occasionally.

Marriage has its seasons, and each season has its changes, advantages and disadvantages, and ups and downs. There are only two things that are permanent: God and change. Everything must change. God will not! Grow/go toward God through the transformation. You will be blessed in the process.

Get Christian counseling. Listen to Moody or Salem Broadcasting's radio teachers. Read *Liberated by Submission* by Bunny Wilson, *The Power of a Praying Wife* **by** Stormie

Chapter 8

Omartian (especially the first chapter), and *Prayers That Avail Much*. by Copeland Germaine. Pray God's Word back to Him. Order tapes and books from the resources listed in the appendix. Read the Bible, seeking help in each page. It's there! Learn who the real enemy is. We do not wrestle against flesh and blood. Fight using prayer and the sword of the Spirit, which is God's Word. Change the only thing over which you have any control—yourself through Christ. Stay in your marriage *and fight the spirit of pride,* not the person you married. He (she) is His child, too. Out of reverence and submission to God, honor the covenant made before the Lord to remain "for better or worse, for richer or poorer, in sickness and health, to love and to cherish, until death do us part." Or, using the Word found in Ephesians 6:13-14: *stand!*

> "And if one prevail against him, two shall withstand him; and a threefold cord is not quickly broken" (Ecclesiastes 4:12).

Read *Romans 12* for more of the basic guidelines of all Christian conduct.

> Behold, I come quickly! Blessed is he that keeps the words of the prophecy of this book.... I am coming quickly and My reward is with Me, to give to every one according to his work. I am the Alpha and the Omega, the Beginning and the End, the First and the Last. (Revelation 22:7, 12-13)
>
> I, Jesus, have sent My angel to testify to you these things in the churches. I am the Root and the Offspring of David, and the Bright and Morning Star. (Revelation 22:16)

Surely I am coming quickly. (Revelation 22:20)

The
B *asic*
I *nstruction*
B *efore*
L *eaving*
E *arth*

"Thy Word have I hid in my heart that I might not sin against thee" (Psalm 119:11).

Jesus "was the true Light, which lighteth every man that cometh into the world" (John 1:9).

"You are the light of the world" (Matthew 5:14).

Chapter 8

"You must be born again." (John 3:3, 5, 7)

Are you experiencing troubling thoughts? Do you want to reprogram our mind? Memorize the ABCs. Other than the Word, in summary, nothing tells who Jesus is better than *The Alpha and The Omega*, written by Mike Gendron, that proclaims the Gospel For those who are seeking and those who know the Truth, It's as simple as A-B-C. Enjoy!

The Alpha and the Omega
by Mike Gendron

Take time to mediate on the Lord Jesus Christ and what He did for us. He is the...

Almighty and Awesome Advocate, abased for aliens, adulterers and alcoholics

Blessed Bread of Life, the Bridegroom bludgeoned and bloodied for His bride

Creator and Christ, crucified on a cross for crooks and criminals
Divine Deity, who descended and died to deliver dirty, depraved degenerates from death
Eternal Emmanuel who endured enmity to enrich His enemies
Faithful and Fairest Forerunner who freely forfeited His life to forgive failures
Glorious God, goaded and gashed to give the Gospel of grace to the guilty
Holy and Heavenly Head who humbled Himself to heal the helpless and hopeless
Incomparable "I AM," the Incarnation of Innocence, insulted for idolaters
Judge and Justifier of the unjust
King of Kings before which every knee shall kneel
Lion and Lamb, Lord and Life, Light and love, lowered to lay down His life for the lost
Majestic Maker, Master and Messiah murdered to mediate mercy to mankind
Name above every name, nailed naked for the nasty and naughty
Only Omnipotent, Omniscient One who overcame for the offenses of outcasts
Perfect and Pure Prince of Peace, Passover and Priest, pierced and persecuted to pardon prodigals, prisoners and prostitutes
Quintessence of Quality, quashed for quarreling quacks
Resurrected Righteous Ruler and Redeemer who resigned His royal residence to ransom and reconcile ruthless rebels
Supreme Savior and Sufficient Substitute, savagely sacrificed to sovereignty secure salvation for the sorriest of sinners

Chapter 8

Testifier of Truth, tortured for thieves, trespassers and transgressors
Unchanging and Uniquely Unblemished One upended for the unworthy and unrighteous
Venerated Vine who verily, verily voiced victory over our vices
Wonderful Word, worthy to be worshiped yet wounded for the worst of the wicked
e**X**alted Example, executed to excuse the excluded
Yahweh, saying yes and yielding to yahoos
Zenith, zealously zapped for zeroes... like me

Satan could not seduce Him, death could not destroy Him, and the grave could not hold Him.
Jesus is our awesome God and all-sufficient Savior!

What Must You Do to be Saved?

**Pray this prayer aloud.
Then sign it.**

Father,
   I confess with my mouth and believe in my heart that Jesus is the Son of God, and that You raised Him from the dead on the third day. I believe He died so I could be forgiven for my sins. I need to be saved from sin, from doubt, from weakness and from cowardly fear. I cannot save myself. Come to live in me so I can learn your ways and gain wisdom and understanding from your Word. I want to be born again—of water and of the Spirit. I ask these things in the Name of Jesus Christ.

   Thank You for salvation,
   I love You,

Name _____

Date _____

The Bible Explained

Want to Know What's Next?

And Jesus came and spoke to them, saying, "All authority (power) has been given unto me in heaven and in earth. Go therefore, and make disciples of all the nations, baptizing them in the name of the Father and of the Son and of the Holy Spirit, teaching them to observe all things that I have commanded you: and lo, I am with you always, even to the end of the world." (Matthew 28:18-20 KJV and NKJV)

There's Power in the Name of Jesus!

"I press toward the goal for the prize of the upward call of God in Christ Jesus." (Philippians 3:14)

The Finish Line Amazing Grace!

Chapter 9

BIBLICAL HELPS & EXERCISES

Help!

"The Lord is my helper, and I will not fear what man shall do to me" (Hebrews 13:6).

The Bible Explained

Where to Find It in the Old Testament

What the Bible says about itself	Ps. 19:7-8
Sustaining faith when facing difficulty	Ps. 27:14
The mercy of God	Ps. 51
Relief in times of illness or trouble	Ps. 91
The remedy for the blues	Ps 34
The nearness of God	Ps. 139
Courage for your work	Josh., ch. 1
A call to faith and repentance	Isa. 55:1-7
Inspiration for greater love for the church	Ps. 84
A pleasant reminder not to forget our blessings	Ps. 103
Why God's Word should be kept alive in the heart	Ps. 119:11
Deliverance from affliction	Ps. 34.19
Help in spiritual blackout	Isa 60:2; Ps. 139:10, 12
Help when despondent	Ps. 43:5; 120:1; Isa. 40:28
Help when discouraged	Isa. 41:10
Freedom from fear	I Sam. 12:24; Ps. 27:1; 118:6
Aid when discontented	Ps. 37:7; Prov. 16:8; Ec. 4:6
Thanksgiving for God's goodness	Ps. 100
A prayer for the day	Ps. 5:3, 8; 51:10; 25:2; 16:1
An inspiring word for the bereaved	Job 1:21; Ec 7:2
How to act in a crisis	Ex. 14:13; Jer. 32:17-18
Prescription for happiness	Ps. 1:1, 2
Aid in sorrow	Ps. 18:6
The source of confidence	Job 34:29; Isa. 30:15
A timely word against idleness	Prov. 24:30, 31; 6:6; 13:4; 22:29
The Ten Commandments	Ex. 20

Chapter 9

The benefits of good companionship	Gen. 5:24; Amos 3:3 Prov. 13:20; 1:10; 4:14
Strength in weakness	Prov. 6:2; Ps. 73:26; Prov. 10:29; Isa. 25:4
Our invisible ally	II Kings 6:17
How to silence gossip	Prov. 26:12–28
When heartbroken	Ps. 102:4, 11; 69:20; 142:3; 28:17
When angry	Ps. 15:1; 16:32
When insincere	Job 31:5–6; Jos. 24:14
Vitamins for the soul	Isa. 55:2
A cure for ignorance	Prov. 9:9; 4:13
The folly of haughtiness	Prov. 16:18
A word about hope	Job 7:6; Ps.119:116; 31:24
Ingratitude	Deut. 8:12, 14
Why we should trust in God	Ps. 46:1
Using what you have	Ex. 4:1–5, 10–13
The peace of fidelity	Ps. 119:161–168
Intemperance	Prov. 20:1; Dan. 1:8
Instability	Jer. 2:36
The danger of vengeance	Prov. 28:10
The value of vision	Prov. 29:18; Jer. 5:21
The king's highway	Isa. 35:8–10
Misunderstanding	Job 3:9,8; Prov. 12:22
Precious promises of God	Ex. 20:2, Ps. 32:8, Josh. 1:5
On guard against flattery	Prov. 29:5; 28:23; 20:19
Misjudgment	I Sam.16:7
The certainty of death	Job 16:22; Ps. 49:15, 23:4
Conscience	Prov. 28:1
Consolation	Ps. 119:50

The Bible Explained

Being honest with yourself	Isa 66:13
Insubordination	Jer. 5:23; I Sam. 15:23; Ps 66:13
Responsibility as an employee	Eccl. 9:10
Obligation of employer	Deut. 24:14, Prov. 22:16; Jer. 22:13
Is there no other way?	II Kings 5:12
Precious jewels of God	Mal 3:17
Boasting	Prov. 27:1-2
Initiative	Num. 13:31, 30; Ps. 126
Injustice	Isa. 59:14, 82:2, Zeph. 3:5
Fool's company	Prov. 13:20
The danger of inferiority complex	Job 7:20, 12:3

Chapter 9

Where to Find It in the New Testament

What the Bible says about itself	Rom. 15:4; II Tim. 3:16–17, Heb. 4:12
Comfort when you are in trouble	John, ch. 14
The cure for worry	Matt. 6:19–34
Strength for your faith	Heb., ch. 11
Jesus' idea of prayer	Matt. 6:5–15; Luke 11:1–13
Paul's idea of Christianity	II Cor. 5:15–19
Paul's rules on how to get along with men	Rom., ch. 12
Rest when you feel weary	Matt. 11:25–30
A remedy for bitterness of spirit	1 Cor., ch. 13
Paul's secret of happiness	Col. 3:12–17
Jesus' idea of a Christian	Matt., ch. 5
The golden text of the Bible	John 3:16
An inspiring word for the bereaved	1 Cor. 15:39–58
Practical religion	James 1:19–27
A message to those who doubt	John 7:17
The golden rule	Luke 6:31
The way to God	John 14:6
The one thing we should do	Phil. 3:13–14
Help in spiritual blackout	John 8:10
Virtues of true character	Phil. 4:8
How to act in a crisis	Rom. 8:28; Luke 22:42
The Beatitudes	Matt. 5:3–12
The Lord's Prayer	Matt. 6:9–13
Help when discouraged	Heb. 13:6; 1 Cor. 16:13
Aid when discontented	Phil 4:11

The Bible Explained

Forgiveness	Matt. 18:21–22; Eph. 4:32; Matt. 6:14; 5:7
The Great Commandments	Matt. 22:37–39
The story of Christmas	Luke 2:8–11, 13–14
The story of Easter	Matt. 28:1–6
The Christian armor	Eph. 6:11–18
The qualities of a good Samaritan	Luke 10:30–37
Victory	I John 5:4
Real religion	1 Cor. 10:2–33
Vitamins for the soul	John 6:22–35
A cure for ignorance	Jas. 1:5; Rom. 11:33
The folly of haughtiness	Matt. 23:12; 1 Cor. 4:7; 10:12
A word about hope	Heb. 6:19; 11:1
The need of patience	Jas. 5:11; Heb. 10:36; Jas. 1:3, 1 Thess. 5:14; Gal. 6:9
Inconsistency	Matt. 7:3–5; Titus 1:16; Rom. 2:21
The danger of vengeance	Rom. 12:09; Matt. 5:44–45
Procrastination	Acts 24:25; John 4:35; Jas. 4:13–14
The value of vision	I Cor. 2–10, 12
Precious promise of Jesus	Matt. 11:28; John 8:31, 32; 6:35; Matt. 28:20
Counterfeit life	Rev. 3:1
Unkindness	Luke 10:30, 32, 34, 36
The joy of a good conscience	Acts. 23:1
The highest loyalty	Matt. 22:37–39
How to approach the throne of grace	Heb. 4:16
Meeting temptation	I Cor. 10:13; Matt. 26:41
Instability	II Pet. 3:17; 1 Cor. 15:58
On guard against flattery	Luke 6:26

Chapter 9

Misjudgment	Rom. 14:10; John 12:47; Matt. 7:1
The certainty of death	Luke 23:46
Conscience	Titus 1:15; Acts 24:16
Consolation	Rom. 15:4; II Cor. 1:3, 4
How to overcome an inferiority complex	I Cor. 15:10; Luke 12:6, 7; Acts 20:32

Write the Ten Commandments
Exodus 20:2–17

1. Thou shalt have

   _____

2. Thou shalt not make

   _____

3. Thou shalt not take

   _____

4. Remember

   _____

5. Honor

   _____

6. Thou shalt not

   _____

7. Thou shalt not

   _____

8. Thou shalt not

   _____

9. Thou shalt not _____

10. Thou shalt not _____

Biblical Numbers Exercise

1. There is one Book of Prophecy _____.

2. The two main divisions (parts) of the Bible, _____ and _____

3. Three parts of the godhead _____, _____ and _____.

4. The four Gospel writers are _____, _____, _____, and _____.

5. The five major prophets: _____, _____, _____, _____, _____.

6. The five books of the law: _____, _____, _____, _____, _____, _____.

7. The five books of Hymns, Literature, and Poetry: _____, _____, _____, _____, _____.

8. The number of Books of the Bible, _____.

Chapter 9

9. The names of seven general letters _____, _____, _____, _____, _____, _____, _____.

10. The longest verse in the Bible is Esther _____:9.

11. Nine Churches received _____ from Paul.

12. The Ten Commandments are found in what two books of the Bible? _____ and _____.

13. Eleven _____ were written for Churches.

14. There were twelve _____ Prophets and History Books.

Write the most important facts you've learned.

_____

_____

_____

_____

_____

_____

_____

_____

_____

Take a Spiritual Gifts Test

God Has Given Spiritual Gifts to Each Person! What are yours?

Think of what you thoroughly enjoy doing. When people compliment you, what do they say? Listen carefully! They may see something in you of which you are unaware. Your work should involve your God-given gift and what you enjoy doing. Make a list of your special gifts. You will be successful and happy.

_____

_____

_____

_____

_____

_____

_____

_____

_____

_____

_____

_____

Chapter 9

WRITE YOUR PRAYER

Remember **ACTS**
(A = Adoration, C = Confession, T = Thanks, S = Supplication or Supply needs or ask/make requests)

Dear Father,

(A) I glorify your Name. (or say I praise your Holy Name.)

(C) Please forgive me for

_____

_____

(T) Thank you for raising Jesus from the tomb on the third day, so I can have everlasting life. Thank you for

_____

_____

(S) Please

_____

_____

Amen

    Since Jesus died on the cross for my sins, I am living my life for God.

The Bible Explained

Appendix

APPENDIX

The Old and New Testament Contents
Psalm and Proverbs References

The Bible Explained

The Contents of the Books of the Old and New Testaments

This entry is a copy from an old, embossed, leather-bound Bible that belonged to the father of my ninety-two-year-old mother-in-law, Gertrude Walker Stigger. The editorial page with the year of publication was missing, due to age and deterioration. Her husband, Mr. John Walker, died at the age of eighty in 1940.

The approximate date of this excerpt is the year 1881

Appendix

GENESIS	Chapter
Creation	1
Formation of Man	2
The Fall	3
Death of Abel	4
Generations of Adam	5
The Ark	6
The Deluge	7
Waters assuaged	8
Death of Noah	9
Noah's generations	10
Babel built	11
Call of Adam	12
Abram and Lot	13
Battle of the Kings	14
Abrams's faith	15
Departure of Hagar	16
Circumcision	17
Abraham and the Angels	18
Destruction of Sodom	19
Abraham denieth Sarah	20
Isaac is born	21
Isaac is offered up	22
Death of Sarah	23
Isaac and Rebecca meet	24
Abraham's death	25
Isaac blessed	26
Jacob and Esau	27
Jacob's vision and vow	28
Jacob marrieth Rachel	29
Birth of Joseph	30
Departure of Jacob	31
Jacob and the Angel	32
Jacob and Esau, etc.	33
Shechemites slain	34
Jacob's altar at Beth-el	35
Generations of Esau	36
Joseph sold by his brothers	37
Judah's incest	38
Joseph and Pharaoh's wife	39
Pharaoh's butler, etc.	40
Pharaoh's dreams	41
Joseph's brothers in Egypt	42
Joseph entertains his brothers	43
Joseph's policy to his brothers	44
Joseph known to his brothers	45
Jacob goeth into Egypt	46
Joseph presents his brother	47
Joseph goeth to his father	48
Jacob blesses his sons	49
Death of Joseph	50

EXODUS	Chapter
The Israelites oppressed	1
Moses born	2
The burning bush	3
God's message to Pharaoh	4
The bondage of the Israelites	5
God's promise renewed	6
Moses goeth to Pharaoh	7
Plague of frogs	8
Plagues continued	9
Plagues continued	10
The Israelites borrow jewels	11
Passover instituted	12
Departure of the Israelites	13
Egyptians drowned	14
The song of Moses	15
Manna and quails sent	16
Moses builds an altar	17
Moses meets his wife and sons	18
God's message from Sinai	19
The Ten Commandments	20
Laws against murder	21
Laws against theft, etc.	22
Laws against false witness, etc.	23
Moses called into the mount	24
Form of the ark	25
Curtains for the ark	26
Altar of burnt-offering	27
Aaron and his sons make priests	28
Priests consecrated	29
Ransom of souls	30
Moses receiveth the two tables	31
Golden Calf. Tables broken	32
God talketh with Moses	33

THE BIBLE His Story (History) EXPLAINED

Tables renewed	34
Free gifts for the Tabernacle	35
People's liberality restrained	36
Ark, Mercy-seat, etc.	37
Sum of the offerings	38
Holy garments made	39
Tabernacle anointed	40

LEVITICUS	**Chapter**
Burnt-offering	1
Meat-offerings	2
Peace-offerings	3
Sin-offerings	4
Trespass-offerings	5
Trespass-offerings	6
Law of trespass-offerings	7
Aaron and his sons consecrated	8
Aaron's sin-offering	9
Nadab and Abihu slain	10
Unclean beasts	11
Purifications	12
Law of leprosy	13
Law for the leper	14
Uncleanness of issues	15
Sin-offerings	16
Blood forbidden	17
Unlawful marriages	18
Repetition of laws	19
Denunciations for sins	20
Priests' qualifications	21
Nature of sacrifices	22
Feasts of the Lord	23
Shelomith's son	24
The Jubilee	25
Obedience required	26
Nature of vows	27

NUMBERS	**Chapter**
The tribes numbered	1
Order of the tribes	2
Levites appointed priests	3
The service of the Kohathites	4
Trial of jealousy	5
Law of the Nazarite	6
Offerings of the princes	7
Levites consecrated	8
Passover commanded	9
The Israelites' march	10
The Israelites loathe manna	11
Miriam's leprosy	12
Delegates search the land	13
The people murmur at the report	14
Sundry laws given	15
Korah, Dathan, Etc., slain	16
Aaron's rod flourisheth	17
Portion of the priests and Levites	18
Law of purification…	19
Moses smiteth the rock	20
Brazen serpent appointed	21
Balak sends for Balaam	22
Balak's sacrifices	23
Balaam's prophesy	24
Zimre and Cozbi slain	25
Israel numbered	26
Death of Moses foretold	27
Offerings to be observed	28
Offerings at feasts	29
Vows not to be broken	30
Midianites spoiled	31
Reubenites and Gadites reproved	32
Journeys of the Israelites	33
Borders of the land appointed	34
Cities of Refuge appointed	35
Gilead's inheritance retained	36

DEUTERONOMY	**Chapter**
Moses rehearseth God's promise	1
Story of the Edomites	2
Moses prayeth to see Canaan	3
An exhortation to obedience	4
Ten Commandments	5
Obedience to the law enjoined	6
Strange communion forbidden	7
God's mercies claim obedience	8
Israel's rebellion rehearsed	9
The tables restored	10

Appendix

An exhortation to obedience	11
Blood forbidden	12
Idolaters to be stoned	13
Of meats, clean and unclean	14
Of the year of release	15
The feast of the Passover	16
The choice and duty of a king	17
The priests' portion	18,
Cities of refuge appointed	19
The priest's exhortation before battle	20
Expiration of uncertain murder	21
Of humanity toward brethren	22
Divers laws and ordinances	23
Of divorce	24
Stripes must not exceed forty	25
Of the offering of first-fruits	26
The law to be written on stones	27
Blessings and curses declared	28
God's covenant with his people	29
Mercy promised to the penitent	30
Moses giveth Joshua a charge	31
The song of Moses	32
The majesty of God	33
Moses vieweth the land and dies	34

JOSHUA	**Chapter**
Joshua succeedeth Moses	1
Rahab concealeth the spies	2
The waters of Jordan divided	3
Twelve stones for a memorial	4
Manna ceaseth	5
Jericho besieged and taken	6
Achan's sin punished	7
Joshua taketh Ai	8
The craft of the Gibeonites	9
The sun and moon stand still	10
Divers kings conquered	11
Names of the conquered Kings	12
Balaam slain	13
The inheritance of the tribes	14
The borders of the lot of Judah	15
Ephraim's inheritance	16

The lot of Manasseh	17
The lot of Benjamin	18
The lot of Simon	19
Cities of refuge, etc.	20
God giveth Israel rest	21
The two tribes and half sent home	22
Joshua's exhortation before his death	23
Joshua's death and burial	24

JUDGES	**Chapter**
The acts of Judah and Simeon	1
The Israelites fall into idolatry	2
The nations left to prove Israel	3
Deborah and Barak deliver Israel	4
The song of Deborah and Barak	5
The Israelites oppressed by Midian	6
Gideon's army	7
The Ephraimites pacified	8
Abimelech made king	9
Tolah judgeth Israel	10
Jephthah's rash vow	11
The Ephraimites slain	12
Samson born	13
Samson's marriage and riddle	14
Samson is denied his wife	15
Delilah's falsehood to Samson	16
Micah's idolatry	17
The Danites seek an inheritance	18
The Levite and his concubine	19
The complaint of the Levite	20
Benjamin's desolation bewailed	21

RUTH	**Chapter**
Elimelech driven into Moab	1
Ruth gleaning in Boaz's field	2
Boaz's bounty to Ruth	3
Boaz's marrieth Ruth	4

FIRST BOOK OF SAMUEL	**Chapter**
Samuel born	1
Hannah's song	2

THE BIBLE His Story (History) EXPLAINED

The Lord calleth Samuel	3	Amnon and Tamar	13
Eli's death	4	Absalom's return	14
Dagon falleth before the ark	5	Absalom's policy	15
The ark sent back	6	Shimei curseth David	16
The Israelites repent	7	Ahithophel hangeth himself	17
The Israelites desire a king	8	Absalom slain by Joab	18
Samuel entertaineth Saul	9	Shimei is pardoned	19
Saul anointed	10	Sheba's revolt	20
The Ammonites smitten	11	Saul's sons hanged	21
Samuels's integrity	12	David's thanksgiving	22
Saul reproved	13	David's faith	23
Saul's victories	14	David numbereth the people	24
Saul spares Agag	15		
Samuel anointeth David	16	**I KINGS**	**Chapter**
David slayeth Goliath…	17	Solomon anointed king	1
Jonathan's love of David…	18	David' death	2
Saul's jealousy of David…	19	Solomon chooseth wisdom	3
David and Jonathan consult…	20	Solomon' prosperity	4
David feigns himself mad…	21	Hiram and Solomon agree	5
Nob destroyed	22	The building of the temple	6
David rescueth Keilah	23	Ornaments of the temple	7
David spareth Saul	24	The temple dedicated	8
The Death of Samuel	25	God's covenant with Solomon	9
David findeth Saul asleep	26	The queen of Sheba	10
David fleeth to Gath	27	Ahijah's prophecy	11
Saul consults a witch	28	The ten tribes revolt	12
Achish dismisseth David	29	Jeroboams's hand withers	13
Amalekites spoil Ziklag	30	Abijah sickness and death	14
Saul and his sons slain	31	Jeroboam's sin punished	15
		Jericho rebuilt	16
II SAMUEL	**Chapter**	The widow's son raised	17
David laments Saul	1	Elijah obtaineth rain	18
David made King of Judah…	2	Elisha followeth Elijah	19
Joab killeth Abner	3	Samaria besieged	20
Ish-bosheth murdered	4	Naboth stoned	21
David's age and reign	5	Ahab seduced	22
Uzzah smitten	6		
God's promise to David	7	**II KINGS**	**Chapter**
David's officers	8	Moab rebeleth	1
David sends for Mephiboseth	9	Elijah's translation	2
Hanun's villainy	10	Moabites defeated	3
David's adultery	11	The widow's oil multiplied	4
Nathan's parable	12	Naaman cleansed	5

Appendix

A famine in Samaria	6	Preparation for the temple	22
Plenty in Samaria	7	Solomon made king	23
Ben-hadad killed	8	The order of Aaron's sons	24
Jezebel eaten by dogs	9	The number of the singers	25
Prophets of Baal slain	10	The division of the porters	26
Jehoash anointed king	11	The twelve captains	27
The temple repaired	12	David's exhortation	28
Elisha's death	13	David's reign and death	29
Amariah reigneth	14		
Azariah's leprosy	15	**II CHRONICLES**	**Chapter**
Ahaz's wicked reign	17	Solomon's offering	1
Rabshakeh's blasphemy	18	Solomon sendeth to Huram	2
Hezekiah's prayer	19	The building of the temple	3
Hezekiah's death	20	The vessels of the temple	4
Manasseh's iniquity	21	The temple finished	5
Huldah's prophesieth	22	Solomon blesseth the people	6
Josiah destroyeth the idolaters	23	Solomon's sacrifice	7
Judah taken captive	24	Solomon buildeth cities	8
The temple destroyed	25	The queen of Sheba visiteth Solomon	9
I CHRONICLES	**Chapter**	Rehoboam made king	10
Adam's line to Noah	1	Judah strengthened	11
The posterity of Israel	2	Rehoboam's reign and death	12
The sons of David	3	Abijah overcometh Jeroboam	13
The posterity of Judah	4	Asa destroyeth idolatry	14
The line of Reuben	5	Asa's covenant with God	15
The sons of Levi	6	Asa's death and burial	16
The sons of Issachar	7	Jehoshaphat's good reign	17
The sons of Benjamin	8	Micaiah's prophesy	18
The genealogies of Israel and Judah	9	Jehoshaphat's care for justice	19
		Jehoshaphat's fast and prayer	20
Saul's overthrow and death	10	Jehoram's wicked reign	21
David made king of Israel	11	Ahaziah's wicked reign	22
The armies that helped David	12	Joash made king	23
David fetcheth the ark	13	Zechariah stoned	24
Hiram's kindness to David	14	The Edomites overcome	25
David bringeth the ark to Zion	15	Uzziah's leprosy	26
David's psalm of thanksgiving	16	Jatham's good reign	27
Nathan's message to David	17	Ahaz's wicked reign	28
David's victories	18	Hezekiah's good reign	29
David's messengers ill-treated	19	The passover proclaimed	30
Rabbah taken and spoiled	20	Provision for the priests	31
The plague stayed	21	Hezekiah's death	32

THE BIBLE His Story (History) EXPLAINED

Manasseh's wicked reign	33
Josiah's good reign	34
Josiah slain in battle	35
Jerusalem destroyed	36

EZRA — Chapter

The proclamation of Cyrus	1
The people return from Babylon	2
The alter erected	3
The decree of Artazerzes	4
Tatnai's letter to Darius	5
The temple finished	6
Ezra goeth to Jerusalem	7
Ezra keepeth a fast	8
Ezra's prayer	9
Ezra's mourning	10

NEHEMIAH — Chapter

Nehemiah mourneth for Jerusalem	1
Artaxerxes encourageth Nehemiah	2
The names of the builders	3
Nehemiah appointeth a watch	4
Reformation of usury	5
Sanballat's practices	6
Hanaani and Hanaaniah's charge	7
The reading of the law	8
A solemn fast appointed	9
The points of the covenant	10
Who dwelt at Jerusalem	11
The high priest's succession	12
Divers abuses reformed	13

ESTHER — Chapter

Ahasuerus's royal feast	1
Esther made queen	2
Haman despised by Mordecai	3
The mourning of the Jews	4
Esther obtaineth the king's favor	5
Mordecai's good services	6
Haman is hanged	7
The rejoicing of the Jews	8
Mordecai's advancement	10

JOB — Chapter

Job's losses and temptations	1
Job smitten with boils	2
Job curseth the day of his birth	3
Eliphaz reproveth Job	4
Afflictions are from God	5
Job wisheth for death	6
Job excuseth his desire of death	7
Bildad sheweth God's justice	8
The innocent often afflicted	9
Job expostulateth with God	10
Zophar reproveth Job	11
God's omnipotence maintained	12
Job's confidence in God	13
The conditions of man's life	14
Eliphaz reproveth Job	15
Job reproveth his friends	16
Job's appeal to God	17
Bildad reproveth Job	18
Job's complaint of his friends	19
The portion of the wicked	20
The destruction of the wicked	21
Job accused of divers sins	22
God's decree is immutable	23
Sin goeth often unpunished	24
Man cannot be justified before God	25
Job reproveth Bildad	26
The hypocrite is without hope	27
Wisdom is the gift of God	28
Job bemoaneth himself	29
Job's honor turned to contempt	30
Job professeth his integrity	31
Elihu reproveth Job	32
Elihu reasoneth with Job	33
God cannot be unjust	34
No comparison with God	35
The justice of God's ways	36
God's great works	37
God's wisdom is unsearchable	38
God's power in His creatures	39
Job humbleth himself to God	40
God's power in the creation	41

Appendix

Job's age and death	42

PSALMS	**Chapter**
Happiness of the Godly	1
The kingdom of Christ	2
The security of God's protection	3
David prayeth for audience	4
David's profession of his faith	5
David's complaint in sickness	6
The destruction of the wicked	7
God's love to man	8
God praised for His judgments	9
The outrage of the wicked	10
God's providence and justice	11
David craveth God's help	12
David boasteth of divine mercy	13
The natural man described	14
A citizen of Zion described	15
David's hope of his calling	16
David's hope and confidence	17
David praiseth God	18
David prays for grace	19
The Church's confidence in God	20
A thanksgiving for victory	21
David's complaint and prayer	22
David's confidence in God's grace	23
God's worship in the world	24
David's confidence in prayer	25
David resorteth unto God	26
David's love to God's service	27
David blesseth God	28
Why God must be honored	29
David's praise for deliverance	30
David rejoiceth in God's service	31
Who are blessed	32
God is to be praised	33
Those blessed who trust in God	34
David prayeth for his safety	35
The excellency of God's mercy	36
David persuadeth to patience	37
David moveth God to compassion	38
The brevity of life	39
Obedience the best sacrifice	40
God's care of the poor	41
David's zeal to serve God	42
David prays to be restored	43
The church's complaint to God	44
The majesty of Christ's kingdom	45
The church's confidence in God	46
The kingdom of Christ	47
The privileges of the church	48
Worldly prosperity condemned	49
God's majesty in the church	50
David's prayer and confession	51
David's confidence in God	52
The natural man described	53
David's prayer for salvation	54
David's complaint in prayer	55
David's promise of praise	56
David in prayer flees to God	57
David describeth the wicked	58
David prayeth for deliverance	59
David's comfort in God's promises	60
David voweth perpetual service	61
No trust in worldly things	62
David's thirst for God	63
David's complaint of his enemies	64
The blessedness of God's chosen	65
David exhorteth to praise God	66
A prayer for God's kingdom	67
A prayer at the removing of the ark	68
David's complaint in affliction	69
David's prayer for the Godly	70
David's prayer for perseverance	71
David's prayer for Solomon	72
The righteous sustained	73
David prayeth for the sanctuary	74
David rebuketh the proud	75
God's majesty in the church	76
David's combat with diffidence	77
God's wrath against Israel	78
The Psalmist's complaint	79
David's prayer for the church	80
An exhortation to praise God	81
David reproveth the judges	82
The church's enemies	83

THE BIBLE His Story (History) EXPLAINED

David longeth for the sanctuary	84	A prayer for the Godly	125
David prayeth for mercies	85	The church prayeth for mercies	126
David's complaint of the proud	86	The virtue of God's blessing	127
The nature and glory of the church	87	Those blessed that fear God	128
David's grievous complaint	88	The haters of the church cursed	129
God's praised for his power	89	God to be hoped in	130
God's providence set forth	90	David professeth his humility	131
The state of the godly	91	David's care for the ark	132
God praised for his great works	92	The benefits of the saints' communion	133
The majesty of Christ's kingdom	93	An exhortation to bless God	134
David's complaint of impiety	94	God praised for His judgments	135
The danger of tempting God	95	God praised for manifold mercies'	136
God praised for his greatness	96	The constancy of the Jews	137
The majesty of God	97	David's confidence in God	138
All creatures exhorted to praise God	98	David defieth the wicked	139
God to be worshipped	99	David's prayer for deliverance	140
God to be praised cheerfully	100	David prayeth for sincerity	141
David's profession of godliness	101	David's comfort in trouble	142
God's mercies to be recorded	102	David complaineth of his grief	143
God blessed for his constancy	103	David's prayer for his kingdom	144
God wonderful in providence	104	God's help to the godly	145
The plagues of Egypt	105	David voweth perpetual praise to God	146
Israel's rebellion	106	God praised for his providence	147
God's manifold providence	107	All creatures should praise God	148
David's confidence in God's	108	God praised for his benefits	149
David's complaint of his enemies	109	God praised upon instruments	150
The kingdom of Christ	110		
God praised for his works	111	**THE PROVERBS**	**Chapter**
The happiness for the godly	112		
God praised for his mercy	113	The use of the proverbs	1
The exhortation to praise	114	The benefit of wisdom	2
The vanity of idols	115	Exhortation to sundry duties	3
David studies to be thankful	116	Persuasions to obedience	4
God praised for his mercy and truth	117	The mischief of whoredom	5
David's trust in God	118	Seven things hateful to God	6
Meditation, prayer, and praise	119	Description of a harlot	7
David prayeth against Doeg	120	The call of wisdom	8
The safety of the Godly	121	The doctrine of wisdom	9
David's joy for the church	122	Virtues and vices contrasted	10–24
The godly's confidence in God	123	Observations about kings	25
The church blesseth God	124	Sundry maxims	26

Appendix

Sundry maxims	27	Babylon threatened	13
Observations of impiety	28	Israel's restoration	14
Of public government	29	The lamentable state of Moab	15
Agur's prayer	30	Moab exhorteth to obedience	16
Lemuel's lesson of chastity	31	Syria and Israel threatened	17
		God's care for His people	18
ECCLESIASTES	**Chapter**	The confusion of Egypt	19
The vanity of all human things	1	Egypt and Ethiopia's captivity	20
Wisdom and folly have one end	2	The fall of Babylon	21
A time for all things	3	The Invasion of Jewry	22
The good of contentment	4	Tyre's miserable overthrow	23
The vanity of riches	5	Judgments of God for sin	24
The conclusion of vanities	6	The prophet praises God	25
Remedies against vanities	7	A song of praise to God	26
Kings are to be respected	8	God's care of His vineyard	27
Wisdom is better than strength	9	Ephraim threatened	28
Of wisdom and folly	10	God's judgment on Jerusalem	29
Directions for charity	11	God's mercies toward His church	30
The preacher's care to edify	12	An exhortation to turn to God	31
		Desolation foreshown	32
THE SONG OF SOLMON	**Chapter**	The privileges of the godly	33
The church's love to Christ	1	God revengeth His church	34
Christ's care of the church	2	The blessings of the gospel	35
The church glorieth in Christ	3	Rabshakeh insulteth Hezekiah	36
The graces of the church	4	Hezekiah's prayer	37
Christ's love for His church	5	Hezekiah's thanksgiving	38
The church's faith in Christ	6	Babylonian captivity foretold	39
The graces of the church	7	The promulgation of the gospel	40
The calling of the Gentiles	8	God's mercies to His church	41
		Christ's mission to the Gentiles	42
ISAIAH	**Chapter**	God comforteth His church	43
Isaiah's complaint of Judah	1	The vanity of idols	44
Christ's kingdom prophesied	2	God calleth Cyrus	45
The oppression of the rulers	3	Idols not to be compared with	
Christ's kingdom a sanctuary	4	God	46
God's judgments for sin	5	God's judgment on Babylon	47
Isaiah's vision of God's glory	6	The intent of prophecy	48
Christ promised	7	Christ sent to the Gentiles	49
Israel and Judah threatened	8	Christ's sufferings and patience	50
The church's joy in Christ's birth	9	The certainty of God's salvation	51
God's judgment on Israel	10	Christ's free redemption	52
The calling of the Gentiles	11	The humiliation of Christ	53
Thanksgiving for God's mercies	12	The church's enlargement	54

THE BIBLE His Story (History) EXPLAINED

The happy state of believers	55
Exhortation to holiness	56
God reproveth the Jews	57
Hypocrisy reproved	58
The covenant of the Redeemer	59
The glory of the church	60
The office of Christ	61
God's promises to His church	62
Christ sheweth His power to save	63
The church's prayer	64
The calling of the Gentiles	65
The growth of the church	66

JEREMIAH	Chapter
The calling of Jeremiah	1
Israel is spoiled for His sins	2
God's mercy to Judah	3
Israel called to repentance	4
God's judgments upon the Jews	5
Enemies sent against Judah	6
Jeremiah's call for repentance	7
The calamities of the Jews	8
Jeremiah's lamentation	9
The vanity of idols	10
God's covenant proclaimed	11
The prosperity of the wicked	12
An exhortation to repentance	13
The prophet's prayer	14
Jeremiah's complaint	15
The utter ruin of the Jews	16
The captivity of Judah	17
The type of the potter	18
The desolation of the Jews	19
Pashur smiteth Jeremiah	20
Nebuchadnezzar's war	21
The judgment of Shallum	22
Restoration of God's people	23
The type of good and bad figs	24
Jeremiah reproveth the Jews	25
Jeremiah is arraigned	26
Nebuchadnezzar's conquests	27
Hananiah's prophecy	28
Jeremiah's letter	29
The return of the Jews	30
The restoration of Israel	31
Jeremiah imprisoned	32
Christ the Branch promised	33
Zedekiah's fate foretold	34
God blesseth the Rechabites	35
Jeremiah's prophecies	36

LAMENTATIONS	Chapter
Jerusalem's misery	1
Israel's misery lamented	2
Sorrows of the righteous	3
Zion's pitiful estate	4
Zion's complaint	5

EZEKIEL	Chapter
Ezekiel's vision	1
Ezekiel's commission	2
Ezekiel eats the roll	3
The type of a siege	4
The type of hair	5
Israel threatened	6
Israel's desolation	7
Vision of jealousy	8
The mark preserved	9
Vision of coals of fire	10
The princes' presumption	11
The type of removing	12
Lying prophets	13
Idolaters exhorted	14
The rejection of Jerusalem	15
God's love to Jerusalem	16
The eagles and the vine	17
Parable of sour grapes	18
Of the lion's whelps	19
Israel's rebellions	20
Prophecy against Jerusalem	21
Jerusalem's sins	22
Aholah and Aholibah	23
Jerusalem's destruction	24
Ammonites threatened	25
The fall of Tyros	26
Tyrus's rich supply	27

Appendix

Zidon threatened	28
The judgment of Pharaoh	29
Desolation of Egypt	30
The glory and fall of Assyria	31
The fall of Egypt	32
Ezekiel admonished	33
God's care of his flock	34
Judgment of Seir	35
Israel comforted	36
Vision of dry bones	37
The malice of Gog	38
Israel's victory over Gog	39
Description of the temple	40
Ornaments of the temple	41
The priests' chambers	42
Return of God's glory	43
The priests reproved	44
Division of the land	45
Finances for the princes	46
Vision of the holy waters	47
Portions of the twelve tribes	48

DANIEL   **Chapter**

Jehoikim's captivity	1
Daniel advanced	2
Shadrach, Meshach, and Abednego	3
Nebuchadnezzar's pride and fall	4
Belshazzar's impious feast	5
Daniel in the lions' den	6
Vision of the four beasts	7
Vision of the ram	8
Daniel's confession	9
Daniel comforted	10
Overthrow of Persia	11
Israel's deliverance	12

HOSEA   **Chapter**

Judgments for whoredom	1
The idolatry of the people	2
The desolation of Israel	3
Judgment threatened	4
Israel a treacherous people	5
Exhortation to repentance	6
Reproof for manifold sins	7
Israel threatened	8
Captivity of Israel	9
Israel's impiety	10
Israel's ingratitude to God	11
Ephraim reproved	12
Ephraim's glory vanished	13
Blessings promised	14

JOEL   **Chapter**

God's sundry judgments	1
Exhortation to repentance	2
God's judgments against his people's enemies	3

AMOS   **Chapter**

God's judgments upon Syria	1
God's wrath against Moab	2
Judgments against Israel	3
God reproveth Israel	4
A lamentation for Israel	5
Israel's wantonness plagued	6
Judgments of the grasshoppers	7
Israel's end typified	8
Israel's restoration promised	9

OBEDIAH   **Chapter**

Edom's destruction for their pride and violence	1

JONAH   **Chapter**

Jonah sent to Nineveh	1
The prayer of Jonah	2
The Ninevites' repentance	3
Jonah repines at God's mercy	4

MICAH   **Chapter**

God's wrath against Jacob	1
Against oppression	2
The cruelty of the princes	3
The church's glory	4
The birth of Christ	5
God's controversy	6

THE BIBLE His Story (History) EXPLAINED

The church's complaint	7

NAHUM	Chapter
The majesty of God	1
God's armies against	2
The ruin of Nineveh	3

HABAKKUK	Chapter
Habakkuk's complaint	1
Judgment on the Chaldeans	2
Habakkuk's prayer	3

ZEPHANIAH	Chapter
God's severe judgments	1
Exhortation to repentance	2
Jerusalem sharply reproved	3

HAGGAI	Chapter
The people reproved	1
Glory of the second temple	2

ZECHARIAH	Chapter
Exhortation to repentance	1
Redemption of Zion	2
The type of Joshua	3
The golden candlestick	4
Curse of thieves	5
Vision of the chariots	6
Captives' inquiry of fasting	7
Jerusalem's restoration	8
The coming of Christ	9
God to be sought unto	10
Destruction of Jerusalem	11
Judah's restoration	12
Jerusalem's repentance	13
Jerusalem's enemies- plague	14

MALACHI	Chapter
Israel's unkindness	1
The priests reproved	2
The majesty of Christ	3
Judgments of the wicked	4

MATTHEW	Chapter
The genealogy of Christ	1
Christ's nativity	2
The preaching of John	3
Christ tempted	4
Christ's sermon on the mount	5
Of alms and prayer	6
Rash judgment reproved	7
Christ's miracles	8
Matthew called	9
The apostles sent forth	10
John sendeth to Christ	11
Blasphemy against the Holy Ghost	12
Parable of the sower	13
John, The Baptist beheaded	14
The scribes reproved	15
The sign of Jonas	16
Transfiguration of Christ	17
Christ teacheth humility	18
Christ healeth the sick	19
The laborers in the vineyard	20
The fig tree cursed	2I
The marriage of the king's son	22
The Pharisees exposed	23
Destruction of the temple foretold	24
Parable of the ten virgins	25
Judas betrayeth Christ	26
Christ crucified	27
Christ's resurrection	28

MARK	Chapter
Baptism of Christ	1
Matthew called	2
The apostles chosen	3
Parable of the sower	4
Christ heals the bloody issue	5
Christ walks on the sea	6
The Syrophoenician woman	7
The multitude fed	8
Jesus transfigured	9
Children brought to Christ	10
The barren fig-tree	11

Appendix

The widow and her two mites	12
The destruction of the temple	13
Peter denieth Christ	14
Crucifixion of Christ	15
Resurrection of Christ	16

LUKE	**Chapter**
Christ's conception	1
Christ's circumcision	2
John's testimony of Christ	3
Christ tempted by Satan	4
Miraculous draught of fishes	5
The twelve apostles chosen	6
Christ's testimony of John	7
Jairus' daughter raised	8
How to attain eternal life	9
Seventy disciples sent out	10
A dumb devil cast out	11
Covetousness to be avoided	12
The crooked woman healed	13
The great supper	14
The prodigal son	15
The unjust steward	16
The power of faith	17
The importunate widow	18
Zaccheus called	19
Parable of the vineyard	20
The widow's two mites	21
Christ condemned	22
Christ's death and burial	23
Christ's resurrection	24

JOHN	**Chapter**
The divinity of Christ	1
Water turned into wine	2
Necessity of regeneration	3
The woman of Samaria	4
The impotent man healed	5
Five thousand fed	6
Christ teacheth in the temple	7
Christ's doctrine justified	8
The blind healed	9
Christ the good shepherd	10

Lazarus raised	11
Christ foretells his death	12
Christ's humility	13
The Comforter promised	14
Christ the true vine	15
Christ warns disciples of sufferings	16
Christ's prayer	17
Jesus betrayed	18
Christ's death and burial	19
Christ's resurrection	20
Christ appeareth to his disciples	21

ACTS	**Chapter**
Matthias chosen	1
Peter's sermon	2
The lame healed	3
Peter and John imprisoned	4
Ananias and Sapphira	5
Seven deacons chosen	6
Stephen stoned	7
Philip planteth a church in Samaria	8
Saul's conversion	9
Peter's vision	10
Peter's defence	11
Herod killeth James	12
Paul preacheth at Antioch	13
Paul stoned	14
Circumcision disputed	15
Timothy circumcised	16
Paul persecuted	17
Paul preacheth at Corinth	18
Exorcists beaten	19
Eutychus raised to life	20
Paul goeth to Jerusalem	21
Paul's defence	22
Paul smitten	23
Paul accused before Felix	24
Paul appealeth to Caesar	25
Agrippa almost a Christian	26
Paul shipwrecked	27
A viper fastens on Paul's hand	28

THE BIBLE His Story (History) EXPLAINED

ROMANS	**Chapter**
Paul greeteth the Romans	1
Who are justified	2
Justification by faith	3
Abraham's faith acceptable	4
Sin and death came by Adam	5
Dying to sin	6
The law not sin	7
What frees from condemnation	8
Calling of the Gentiles	9
Paul's prayer for Israel	10
All Israel are not cast off	11
Love required	12
Love the fulfilling of the law	13
How to use Christian liberty	14
The intent of the Scriptures	15
Paul's salutations	16

I CORINTHIANS	**Chapter**
Dissensions of Corinth	1
The wisdom of God	2
Teachers responsibility	3
Servants of Christ	4
A case for church discipline	5
Lawsuits; Warning against laxity	6
Sanctity of marriage	7
Food offered to idols	8
Paul's self-denial	9
Exhortation to righteous living	10
The Lords supper directions	11
Spiritual Gifts	12
The way of love	13
Speaking in tongues	14
The resurrection of Christ	15
Exhortation, greeting, benediction	16

II CORINTHIANS	**Chapter**
Consolation in trouble	1
Paul's success in preaching	2
The excellency of the gospel	3
The Christian's paradox	4
Paul assured of immortality	5
Exhortations to purity	6
Godly sorrow profitable	7
Liberality extolled	8
Bounty praised	9
Paul's spiritual might	10
Paul's godly boasting	11
Paul's revelations	12
Paul's charge	13

GALATIANS	**Chapter**
Of their leaving the gospel	1
Peter reproved	2
Justification by faith	3
Christ freeth us from the law	4
The liberty of the gospel	5
Lenity recommended	6

EPHESIANS	**Chapter**
Of election and adoption	1
Christ our peace	2
The hidden mystery	3
Exhortation to unity	4
Exhortation to love	5
The Christian Armor	6

PHILIPPIANS	**Chapter**
Paul's prayer to God	1
Exhortation to humility	2
All loss for Christ	3
General exhortations	4

COLOSSIANS	**Chapter**
Christ described	1
Exhortation to constancy	2
Household duties	3
Prayer recommended	4

I THESSALONIANS	**Chapter**
History of their conversion	1
How the gospel was preached to the Thessalonians	2
Paul's love in sending Timothy	3
Exhortation to godliness	4
Description of Christ's coming	5

Appendix

II THESSALONIANS	Chapter
Comfort against persecution	1
Of steadfastness in the truth	2
To avoid idleness	3

I TIMOTHY	Chapter
False teacher warning	1
Ordinances regarding worship	2
Concerning bishops and deacons	3
False teachers	4
Directions for the pastor	5
Final directions	6

II TIMOTHY	Chapter
Paul's love to Timothy	1
Exhortation to Timothy	2
All Scripture inspired	3

TITUS	Chapter
Qualifications for ministers	1
Christian' duty	2
Paul directeth what to teach and what not	3

PHILEMON	Chapter
Philemon's faith commended	1

HEBREWS	Chapter
Christ far above angels	1
Obedience due to Christ	2
Christ above Moses	3
The Christian's rest	4
Of Christ's priesthood	5
The danger of apostasy	6
Melchisedek and Christ	7
A new covenant	8
The sacrifices of the law	9
Christ's perfect sacrifice	10
The power of faith	11
Divers exhortations	12
Obedience to spiritual rulers	13

JAMES	Chapter
Wisdom to be sought of God	1
Of faith and works	2
The truly wise	3
Against covetousness	4
The trial of faith	5

I PETER	Chapter
Of God's spiritual graces	1
Christ the cornerstone	2
Duty of wives and husbands	3
Of ceasing from sin	4
The duty of elders	5

II PETER	Chapter
Exhortation to duties	1
False teachers foretold	2
Certainty of judgment	3

I JOHN	Chapter
Christ's person described	1
Christ our advocate	2
God's great love	3
Try the spirits	4
The three witnesses	5

II JOHN	Chapter
An elect lady exhorted	1

III JOHN	Chapter
Gaius' piety commended	1

JUDE	Chapter
Of constancy in the faith	1

REVELATION	Chapter
Of the coming of Christ	1
Balaam's doctrine	2
The key of David	3
The vision of a throne	4
The book with seven seals	5
The seven seals opened	6
The number of the sealed	7

THE BIBLE His Story (History) EXPLAINED

Seven angels with trumpets	8
A star falleth from heaven	9
The book eaten	10
The two witnesses	11
The red dragon	12
The beast with seven heads	13
The harvest of the world	14
The seven angels/seven plagues	15
Of the vials of wrath	16
The scarlet whore	17
The fall of Babylon	18
The lamb's marriage	19
The first resurrection	20
The heavenly Jerusalem described	21
The Tree of Life	22

Appendix

Psalms and Proverbs

PSALMS (Hymns)

A manual and guide and model for the devotional needs of the individual believer, Psalms is a book of prayer and praise. This book truly magnifies God and the Word of God. Its intrinsic spiritual depth and beauty have made it from earliest times a treasury of resources for public and private devotions.

Prayers For...

Deliverance from Personal Enemies: 3-5, 7, 8-10, 12-13, 17, 25, 28, 31,
35, 54-57, 59, 63-64, 69-71, 86, 89, 94, 109, 120, 123, 139-144
Thanksgiving for Deliverance from Personal Enemies: 92
Curse upon enemies (to counteract the effect of a curse): 58 (with caution) 109:17-19
Deliverance from Personal Trouble: 77, 130
Thanksgiving for Deliverance from Trouble: 32, 40, 138
Thanksgiving for Deliverance in battle: 118
Confidence in God's Concern for Justice: 11, 73
Prayer for Protection: 61 Confidence in God's Protection: 62
Deliverance from National Enemies: 44, 60, 74, 79-80, 83, 85, 90, 108,
124-126, 129
The Certainly of Retribution for the Wicked: 37. 50, 52, 58
Prayer for Deliverance from Mortal Illness: 22
Healing from Sickness: 6, 38-39, 41-43, 88, 102 Thanksgiving for Recovery from Sickness: 30, 103 Thanksgiving for Healing: 32, 116
Healing and Moral Renewal (a lament): 51 Prayer for Victory in Battle: 20 Thanksgiving for Victory in Battle: 21
Praise Thanksgiving: 33, 40, 47-48, 65-67, 75, 100, 104, 107, 113, 135-

136, 145-150
A Liturgy of Blessing: 121
Praising Zion as the Pilgrims Goal: 122, 132
A Safe Home and A Large Family — God's Gift: 127, 128 Joys of Fraternal Harmony: 133
Hymn to the God of the Storm: 29
As Creator of Nature: 19
Meditation on the Transience of Life and Wealth: 49
Act of Humble Submission to God's Will and Guidance: 131
Condemnation of a Cynical and Unrighteous Age: 14. 53, 82, 115
God's Kingship: 93, 95-99
The Contrasting Fate of the Righteous and the Wicked: 1, 112 Meditation on God as the Protector of the Faithful: 91
Confidence in God's Protection: 23
The Lord gives Universal Dominion to His King: 2
Hymn Celebrating God's Glory and Man's God-given Dignity: 8 A King gives Thanks for a Victory in Battle: 18
A Liturgy on Entering the Sanctuary: 24
Gods Great Deeds and His People's Faithfulness: 78,105, 106, 111 Meditation on The Law of God: 119
Personal Faith in God's Power to Save (a Song of Trust): 16
Doxology: 117

PROVERBS (A Wisdom Book)

The book of Proverbs is a summary of moral and religious instruction. The purpose of the teacher in assembling the work is to serve the mental awakening and moral education of youth, and the further instruction of the mature. Its emphasis is on moral integrity based on religion, its teaching that reward and punishment follow in this life, its appeal to the lessons of experience rather than revelation, and its exploration of the nature of wisdom and of wisdom's relation to God.

Appendix

The Purpose: 1:2–6
Home Training is a Moral Safeguard: 1:8–19 The Fruits of the Search for Wisdom: 2:1–22 For Physical and Spiritual Well-being: 3:1–12
Peace of Mind through Confidence in God: 3:21–35 Profit by the lessons taught: 4:10–19
Grave warnings against sexual indulgence and marital infidelity: 5:1- 23
Commendation of training in wisdom, with a stern warning against adultery: 6:20–35
Wisdom speaks as a prophetess: 1:20–33, 8:1–36 A Poetic Allegory: 9:1–6
Truths on scoffers and Wise Men: 9:7–12
Folly, in contrast to the Lady Wisdom, is a prostitute leading men to death: 9:13–18
Proverbs of Solomon dealing with virtues and vices and their consequences: 10:1–22:16, and 25:1–29:27
A Queen Mother's Counsel: 31:1–9
The Ideal Housewife: 31:10–31

Psalm and Proverbs Categorized and Summarized by Edna Stigger from the annotations in The New Oxford Annotated Bible, expanded edition, Revised Standard Version

Bibliography

The Holy Ghost, *The Bible*; (Several Versions, Eternity)

Henrietta C. Mears, *What The Bible Is All About*; (Ventura, CA, Regal Books, A Division of GL Publications, 1983)

The Alpha and the Omega written by Evangelist Mike Gendron, Proclaiming The Gospel, a ministry founded for the purpose of leading those Roman Catholics who are unsaved to a saving faith in Jesus Christ.

Then Sings My Soul by Robert J. Morgan is a collection of Christmas, Easter, and All-time Favorite Hymn Stories that also includes the music and lyrics of the hymns so that the reader can immediately see the correlation between the stories and the songs themselves.

The writers of *Our Daily Bread*, for the inspiration and insight gained throughout many years of reading and meditation.

The illustration of the knight in the **Spiritual Protection Explained** chapter is courtesy of artist, Trina Schart Hyman and Harcourt Brace Jovanich, Inc. Orlando, FL. Used with permission.

About the Author

EDNA STIGGER TEACHES Bible History for the Quality Living Services Center for Seniors, at Christian Education forums and among Bible study groups of various denominations. She has taught Sunday School for more than forty years. She is a member of Cascade United Methodist Church, Atlanta, Georgia, where she teaches middle grades Sunday School, and Spiritual Gifts for the Discipleship Ministry New Member Orientation. She has taught Back to Bible Basics Classes using the principles from **The Bible Explained**. (See YouTube video.)

Ms. Stigger graduated from the University of Louisville School of Medical Technology with a BS, and was registered with the American Society of Clinical Pathology (ASCP), specializing in Microbiology at Louisville Children's Hospital. She has completed courses at West Georgia State University in preparation for a master's degree in middle grades education. A former retail business owner and Atlanta Public School teacher, she is presently employed by the Fulton County Department of Health, as Public Health Educator for the Environmental Health Services Division.

Her other books are **Spiritual Journal,** a supplement to The Bible Explained, and **For Wives Only... or Any Woman Who Dares**, subtitled: An eX Strong-Willed Wife's Conversion Vividly Told Through Stories, Prose & Poetry. It chronicles her spiritual adventure which began with her life-changing born-again experience. She shares personal testimonies, prose and poetry given her by the

Holy Spirit as she matured during life altering trials and tribulations.

An enduring, good marriage is qualification for her God-given Titus 2 ministry. Download the introduction at **www.ForWivesOnly.com.**

Of all her professions, she receives the most joy from writing and teaching youth and seniors. She especially enjoys teaching about spiritual warfare and how to dress in the whole armor of God, Jesus Christ. "Holy, Holy, Holy" inspired the Trinity instruction, and her favorite theme song, sung by Marilyn McCoo, states her desire to be a "Warrior for the Lord." Her YouTube video, *The Bible Explained* blesses those who view it.

As a teacher, writer, and caregiver, Edna Stigger shares her spiritual gifts with others, as all her writings are for education, edification, and evangelization.

Edna and Charles Stigger have been married fifty-four years. They have three children, Charles, Lisa, and Cagney, and two grandchildren, Scott and Chanelle Stigger.